Jane Austen

'My Dear Cassandra'

Jane Austen

'My Dear Cassandra'

Selected and Introduced by Penelope Hughes-Hallett

COLLINS & BROWN

FRONT COVER *'Brompton 1822'*
by George Scharf.

BACK COVER *Silhouette of Jane*
Austen, c.1801; a letter
to Cassandra.

Published in Great Britain by
Collins & Brown Limited
London House
Great Eastern Wharf, Parkgate Road
London SW11 4NQ

First published in 1990

Copyright © Collins & Brown 1990

Introduction and commentary copyright
© Penelope Hughes-Hallett 1990

A CIP catalogue record for this book
is available from the British Library

3 5 7 9 8 6 4

ISBN 1 85585 004 4
(ISBN 1 85585 015 X hardback edition)

Conceived, edited and designed by Collins & Brown Limited

Editorial Director: Gabrielle Townsend
Editor: Elizabeth Drury
Picture Research: Philippa Lewis
Art Director: Roger Bristow
Designer: Ruth Hope

Filmset by Goodfellow & Egan, Cambridge
Reproduction by Scantrans, Singapore
Printed and bound in Hong Kong

FRONTISPIECE *Sydney Gardens,*
from John Claude Nattes' Bath.
The gardens were a centre of
much gaiety: concerts, fireworks
and galas. 'There is a public
breakfast in Sydney Gardens
every morning, so that we shall
not be wholly starved,' wrote Jane.

TITLE PAGE *The silhouette found*
pasted into the second edition of
Mansfield Park *and inscribed*
l'aimable Jane.

CONTENTS

THE LETTERS OF JANE AUSTEN

● ● ●

In 1817, a few months after Jane Austen's death, her brother Henry included extracts from two of her letters as a postscript to his 'Biographical Notice of the Author' published in the first volume of the first edition of *Northanger Abbey*. In 1870 her nephew, James Edward Austen-Leigh, published *A Memoir of Jane Austen*, enlarged and revised in the following year, and in this he included some of her letters.

Then, in 1884, Edward, Lord Brabourne published *The Letters of Jane Austen* in two volumes. These were letters that had been bequeathed to Lady Knatchbull (née Fanny Knight), his mother, by her great-aunt Cassandra Austen. It was to Jane's sister Cassandra that most of the letters that survive were written.

By 1884 Jane Austen's novels were much acclaimed. *Sense and Sensibility* had been published in 1811, *Pride and Prejudice* in 1813, *Mansfield Park* in 1814 and *Emma* in 1816; *Northanger Abbey* and *Persuasion* were published posthumously in 1818. The time had come to offer to the public 'a picture of her such as no history written by another person could give so well,' wrote Lord Brabourne. 'Amid the most ordinary details and most commonplace topics, every now and then sparkle out the same wit and humour which illuminate the pages of "Pride and Prejudice", "Mansfield Park", "Emma", etc., and which have endeared the name of Jane Austen to many thousands of readers in English-speaking homes.' This is reason enough to publish a fresh selection of extracts from the letters in an easily readable edition in which relevant excerpts from the novels, together with appropriate illustrations, illuminate Jane Austen the woman and Jane Austen the author.

RIGHT *Painting by John Cordrey of a stage coach, early nineteenth century. These coaches were considered inappropriate for young ladies travelling alone. 'I want to go in a stage coach, but Frank will not let me,' Jane complained.*

INTRODUCTION

On 9 January 1796 Jane Austen took up her pen to write to her elder sister Cassandra. Her twenty-year-old voice, young, confident, laughing, effortlessly crosses the distance of time lying between then and now. She expected her sister would like to know more about her flirt of the moment, and the present-day reader, already under her spell, would too. He 'has but *one* fault, which time will, I trust, entirely remove – it is that his morning coat is a great deal too light.' She was absolute master of the throwaway line, and the wicked delight she took in teasing her sister is infectious.

In 1817, on her deathbed, the by then middle-aged voice had modulated into a serene maturity, informed with endearing modesty and love. To her nephew Edward she wrote, 'If ever you are ill, may you be as tenderly nursed as I have been, may the same blessed alleviations of anxious, sympathising friends be yours, and may you possess – as I dare say you will – the greatest blessing of all, in the consciousness of not being unworthy of their love. *I* could not feel this.'

The surviving, or at least known, letters of the intervening years, most of them written to Cassandra, are delightful and illuminating. They enhance the reader's knowledge of Jane Austen, her attitudes, character, relationships; and also her external circumstances, her extended family circle, the houses in which she passed her life, the manner of that life itself. They recreate the minute fabric of such a life: money, the weather, gardening, the price of fish. All the mundane, trivial things add up to an impression of the actual, made fascinating by the genius of their author.

ABOVE *Drawing by Thomas Rowlandson of a grocer's stall. Then, as now, marketing required an ability to drive a shrewd bargain, in which activity Jane seems, for the most part, to have been skilled.*

Because Cassandra and Jane were seldom, if ever, separated in their childhood and adolescence, the correspondence between them did not begin until Jane was grown up. After that they were frequently apart, and Jane dispatched journal letters to her sister almost twice a week. By then their relationship was so close and harmonious that each was almost an extension of the other. In one letter to Cassandra Jane wrote, 'I have now attained the true art of letter-writing, which we are always told, is to express on paper exactly what one would say to the same person by word of mouth; I have been talking to you almost as fast as I could the whole of this letter'; and indeed her voice, lucid and immediate, gives the reader a beguiling illusion of privileged intimacy.

Jane Austen's strength lay in a shrewd and piercingly accurate examination of provincial life, and her letters demonstrate how much she relished this. In *Emma* the heroine, watching the small happenings in the village street, reflected, 'A mind lively and at ease, can do with seeing nothing, and can see nothing that does not answer', and this also seems an apt comment on Emma's creator. Although the letters were for the most part the record of seemingly unimportant details, these were transmuted by Jane's art into something of precious worth. Sir Walter Scott described her gift as 'that exquisite touch which renders ordinary commonplace things and characters interesting'. Whether she was deploring the necessity of dealing with legs of mutton and doses of rhubarb, or admiring Cowper's poems, or making sharply barbed comments on a hapless acquaintance (as, 'Mrs. Blount . . . with the same broad face, diamond bandeau, white shoes, pink husband, and fat neck'); whether commiserating on a death or triumphantly revamping an evening cap, everything she touched acquired significance. 'I hope George was pleased with my designs', she wrote of a small nephew. 'Perhaps they would have suited him as well had they been less elaborately finished; but an artist cannot do anything slovenly.' The tone may be a laughing one, but the truth of her remark is evident throughout.

ABOVE *'Travelling through Kennington' by Samuel Howitt. A typical eighteenth-century village scene, complete with post-chaise and carrier's wagon. Such a sight would have been familiar to Jane Austen.*

ABOVE *'The Baker', showing a baker delivering his wares in a small country village.*

The particular society her letters evoke is one in which a sense of family is paramount, and indeed in the world of the letters Jane Austen was to some extent defined by family relationships: as a dutiful and loving daughter, especially close to her civilised, sympathetic father; as a dear sister to her tribe of brothers; above all, in her relationship with her beloved Cassandra. The letters served to reinforce this family closeness, as news and messages were relayed from one branch to another. 'My brother', she wrote to Cassandra on 11 October 1813, 'desires his best love and thanks for all your information. Have you any idea of returning with him to Henrietta St. and finishing your visit then? Tell me your sweet little innocent ideas.'

As time passed, Jane was also shown to be an amused and interested aunt. The tone in which she wrote to her favourite nieces and her nephew Edward was markedly different from the private voice reserved for Cassandra, which spoke with such sharply focused insight, creating minutely perfected vignettes, and the famous epigrammatic characterisations. To her young relations she wrote more fluently and easily, with her own special blend of loving advice and gentle ridicule, her topics ranging from love and marriage to the craft of writing novels. Today's reader cannot but be entranced.

Part of the fascination of the letters lies in their power to satisfy that basic curiosity about the author of much-loved works, in order, in some sense, to possess these more fully. And indeed the correspondence does reveal much of the raw material from which the novels were fashioned. Jane's happy letters about the promotions and successes of her sailor brothers bring to mind Fanny Price's delight in William's parallel triumphs in *Mansfield Park*. The closeness of the bond between pairs of sisters – Elinor and Marianne Dashwood in *Sense and Sensibility*, or Jane and Eliza Bennet in *Pride and Prejudice* – lends further emphasis to the impression given by the letters of the loving concord between Cassandra and Jane herself. The lyrical

description of the Dorset countryside in *Persuasion* stems from the same experiences as Jane's lively letter from Lyme, with its talk of walking home in the moonlight from a ball.

The unmarried Jane Austen's dependent state finds echoes in the plight of the various impoverished spinsters mentioned with compassion and concern in her letters. 'Single women have a dreadful propensity for being poor, which is one very strong argument in favour of matrimony', she remarked in one letter. Strong, perhaps, but not sufficiently so; and in another she emphasised this. 'Anything is to be preferred or endured rather than marrying without affection.' She herself gave the impression of preferring a single state in a number of ways. 'Good Mrs. Deedes!' she remarked to her young unmarried niece, Fanny Knight, with earthy realism, 'I hope she will get the better of this Marianne, and then I would recommend to her and Mr. D. the simple regimen of separate rooms.'

The measure of financial independence which accompanied her success as a writer was consequently all the more welcome, and enjoyed without inhibition. Writing to Fanny Knight about a possible second edition of *Mansfield Park*, Jane deplored that 'People are more ready to borrow and praise, than to buy – which I cannot wonder at; but tho' I like praise as well as anybody, I like what Edward calls *Pewter* too.' By the end of her life her earnings from the novels amounted to just over six hundred and eighty pounds.

Jane Austen has sometimes been portrayed as spending her life in the provincial backwater of a country parsonage, but her correspondence shows more varied and sophisticated scenes as she moved around on visits from one country house to another, or enjoyed fashionable London parties, staying with her brother Henry and his lively wife Eliza; the latter's cosmopolitan circle dated from her marriage to the comte de Feuillide, guillotined in 1794. The illustrations to this edition underline the variety of her experience.

BELOW *John Meirs' silhouette of Cassandra, Jane's eldest sister, in her late 30s. 'Take care of your precious self,' wrote Jane, in the tender tone characteristic of their mutual devotion.*

Jane Austen's life spanned the French Revolution and on through the Napoleonic Wars, ending two years after the Battle of Waterloo. Such large events do not feature prominently in intimate domestic letters, but they are reflected in Jane's concern for her two naval brothers, both engaged on active service with the British fleet, and also in references to the miseries of the Peninsular Campaign. 'How horrible it is to have so many people killed', she writes on one occasion; and later, 'Thank Heaven! we have had no one to care for particularly among the troops.'

The novelist's creative life falls into three more or less clearly defined periods: the happy Steventon years when she wrote the first versions of *Sense and Sensibility* and *Pride and Prejudice*; then a long time (the years of Bath and Southampton) when apparently nothing was written. This can perhaps be thought of as a period of accruing experiences and gestation of ideas. The Bath scenes for *Northanger Abbey* and *Persuasion* largely derived from that time; and similarly the Portsmouth scenes in *Mansfield Park* stemmed from her knowledge of Southampton naval life. Then followed the great creative period, the years at Chawton when she was once again happy and able to write, and which saw the publication of four of the six novels, and the completion of *Northanger Abbey* and *Persuasion*, which would be published posthumously in 1818.

Reading the correspondence with this framework in mind gives it an extra dimension, and some of the most engaging letters are those retailing varied reactions to the novels. Jane, not surprisingly, felt partisan about these. 'I want to tell you that I have got my own darling child from London', she wrote on the arrival of the first copy of *Pride and Prejudice*; and, later in the same letter, referring to a friend, Miss Benn, to whom she had been reading the novel, 'she really does seem to admire Elizabeth. I must say that *I* think her as delightful a creature as ever appeared in print, and how I shall be able to tolerate those who do not like *her* at least, I do not know.'

BELOW *Jane's handwriting addressing a letter to Cassandra, who was staying with her brother Henry Austen in London.*

BELOW *Letter to Cassandra written from Manydown. 'Oh! dear me! I have not time or paper for half that I have to say.'*

In making this selection from the letters my purpose has been to present a rounded picture of their author, showing her from as many angles as possible, in many and various moods, from the 'light bright and sparkling' aspect of her young womanhood, the mocking, brilliant ironic voice with the sometimes dangerously cutting edge; the generous rejoicing voice at the good fortune of others; the modesty in face of growing success; the gentle reflective voice of the last sad year, which, however, still remained capable of flashes of the famous ironic wit. Eliza Bennet's claim to Mr. Darcy, 'I hope I never ridicule what is wise or good. Follies and nonsense, whims and inconsistencies do divert me, I own, and I laugh at them whenever I can', would not ring altogether convincingly if applied to the volatile Jane of the Steventon days, but seems appropriately in accord with the voice of her maturity; and this emphasises the poignant distance between the volatile girl and the calm, suffering woman.

The letters have been arranged chronologically in six sections, marking various milestones in Jane Austen's life. These conveniently also coincide with the sequence of her different homes, beginning at Steventon Rectory in Hampshire; on to Bath on her father's retirement; then Southampton after his death. The next two sections are devoted to the Chawton years, and the final one covers the short year of her decline, spent partly at Chawton and then in the Winchester lodgings where she died. The short extracts from the novels that punctuate the text here and there will, it is hoped, serve to highlight links between Jane's life, letters and art.

One reward of reading these captivating letters, with their wit, warmth and poignancy, is that Jane Austen the novelist becomes also Jane Austen the woman, to be regarded not only with an endorsed admiration, but also with a sense of affectionate friendship.

PENELOPE HUGHES-HALLETT

Early Creative Years

LEFT *Samuel Grimm's watercolour of the Hampshire countryside at Selborne. An evocative reminder of the landscape so dear to Jane.*

The first twenty-five years of Jane Austen's life were spent at Steventon Rectory, her father's pleasant rural living in the north Hampshire countryside between Winchester and Basingstoke. Here she grew up surrounded by the affection of an exceptionally closely-knit, talented family, of which she was the seventh child and second daughter. Her sister Cassandra, nearly three years the elder of the two, was her much-loved especial confidante, and it is to her that the greater part of the correspondence is addressed. Fortunately for us, though to their mutual regret, family demands imposed frequent separations upon the sisters, and when apart they usually wrote to each other twice a week.

In 1796, the date the twenty-year-old Jane's letters begin, her father, the Reverend George Austen, was rector of Steventon and of nearby Deane. He was tall, good-looking, with prematurely white shining curls – said to be so striking that when he removed his hat in the streets of Bath people turned to stare. He was a profound scholar, gentle and kindly, with a wry sense of humour. Jane later spoke of his 'sweet benevolent smile'. He created an atmosphere at the Rectory of cultivated rationality which was complemented by Mrs. Austen's qualities of sharp practicality, common sense, sparkling wit and acute perception.

Jane inherited a happy mixture of her parents' characteristics. She was remembered by her nephew, James Austen-Leigh, as 'tall and slender, her step light and firm . . . she had full round cheeks, with mouth and nose small and well formed, light hazel eyes, and brown hair forming natural curls close round her face.'

ABOVE *Jane's first home, Steventon Rectory, drawn by her niece Anna Lefroy in 1820.*

Of the Austen sons, the eldest, James, already a widower, was curate at Deane, and would marry for the second time during the following year. His daughter Anna later became a great favourite with her Aunt Jane; and his son James Edward was destined to be her first biographer, helped in this task by the memories of his younger sister Caroline.

The second son, George, suffered from some disability and never lived with the family. Next came Edward, who was adopted as a boy by his cousins, the rich but childless Thomas Knights of Godmersham Park in Kent, who made him their heir. After Mr. Knight's death and his widow's retirement to a house in Canterbury, Edward moved into Godmersham and assumed the name of Austen Knight. His parents and sisters stayed with him there in 1798. Such visits to the great country house, with all the attendant journeyings and gaieties, were to play an important role in enriching the novelist's experience of society. In 1796, however, Edward and his wife Elizabeth (Bridges) were still living at Rowling, a small country house near her home, Goodnestone.

Henry, reputedly Jane's favourite brother, would become first a banker, later a parson; but at this time he was in the Oxfordshire Militia, and would shortly marry his cousin Eliza de Feuillide.

Francis and Charles, the two younger brothers, were in the Navy, and the next few years would see them involved in the Napoleonic Wars. News of their movements, successes and promotions was eagerly received and discussed. Their careers were distinguished, both eventually becoming admirals.

Although the light and racy tone of these early letters suggests untroubled skies, there were sorrows to contend with. The comte de Feuillide, Eliza Hancock's first husband, had been guillotined in 1794; and, in 1797, Cassandra's fiancé Tom Fowle died from fever in San Domingo. Cassandra never married.

By 1796, with three manuscript volumes of juvenilia to her credit, Jane was already writing novels. *Elinor and Marianne*, later to become *Sense and Sensibility*, was by now completed,

possibly in epistolary form; and by August 1797 she had written *First Impressions*, the original of *Pride and Prejudice*. Mr. Austen, impressed with the novel, sent it to a publisher, who rejected it unread. Jane next began work on *Susan* (posthumously published as *Northanger Abbey*).

The letters give a strong sense of family security and contentment. Mr. Austen read Cowper aloud in the evenings; there was much talk of dressmaking and bonnet refurbishment; Basingstoke Assemblies were enjoyed; parishioners were visited; the rectory pig was killed; weddings were discussed and births rejoiced over or deplored. Such was the fabric of Steventon life.

During the autumn of 1800 Mr. Austen suddenly decided to retire from his livings, possibly for reasons of health. Returning with her friend Martha Lloyd from a visit to the latter at Ibthorpe, Jane was abruptly greeted by Mrs. Austen: 'Well, girls, it is all settled, we have decided to leave Steventon and go to Bath.' It is said that Jane fainted away in the hall at the shock of this news. The blow was a major one: to be forced to leave her beloved Steventon, the tranquil Hampshire countryside, her friends, relations and all the familiar sights of her twenty-five-year-old life; to settle in Bath, bound in by houses, town noise and tiresome provincial town society, was a terrible grief for one of her susceptibilities. In her letter of 3 January 1801 it is hard to say whether she had become reconciled to her lot, or was concealing despair behind a brilliant but brittle façade.

BELOW *A view of Bath from the Bristol Road showing the city's burgeoning terraces and crescents.*

STEVENTON: SATURDAY JANUARY 9 [1796]

ABOVE *Miniature of Tom Lefroy. Tom and Jane flirted with one another. 'He is a very gentlemanlike, good-looking, pleasant young man,' Jane wrote reassuringly to Cassandra.*

BELOW AND RIGHT *'The Five Positions of Country Dancing' from Thomas Wilson's* An Analysis of Country Dancing, *1811. Dancing was considered something of an art. 'We dined at Goodnestone and in the evening danced two country dances and the boulangeries,' Jane reported to her sister.*

*I*N THE FIRST PLACE I hope you will live twenty-three years longer. Mr. Tom Lefroy's birthday was yesterday, so that you are very near of an age.

After this necessary preamble I shall proceed to inform you that we had an exceeding good ball last night . . .

We were so terrible good as to take James in our carriage, though there were three of us before; but indeed he deserves encouragement for the very great improvement which has lately taken place in his dancing. Miss Heathcote is pretty, but not near so handsome as I expected. Mr. H. began with Elizabeth, and afterwards danced with her again; but *they* do not know how *to be particular*. I flatter myself, however, that they will profit by the three successive lessons which I have given them.

You scold me so much in the nice long letter which I have this moment received from you, that I am almost afraid to tell you how my Irish friend and I behaved. Imagine to yourself everything most profligate and shocking in the way of dancing and sitting down together. I *can* expose myself, however, only *once more*, because he leaves the country soon after next Friday, on which day we *are* to have a dance at Ashe after all. He is a very gentlemanlike, good-looking, pleasant young man, I assure you. But as to our having ever met, except at the three last balls, I cannot say much; for he is so excessively laughed at about me at Ashe, that he is ashamed of coming to Steventon, and ran away when we called on Mrs. Lefroy a few days ago . . .

We had a visit yesterday morning from Mr. Benjamin Portal, whose eyes are as handsome as ever. Everybody is extremely anxious for your return, but as you cannot come home by the Ashe ball, I am glad that I have not fed them with false hopes. James danced with Alethea, and cut up the turkey last night with great perseverance . . .

After I had written the above, we received a visit from Mr. Tom Lefroy and his cousin George. The latter is really very well-behaved now; and as for the other, he has but *one* fault, which time will, I trust, entirely remove – it is that his morning coat is a great deal too light. He is a very great admirer of Tom Jones, and therefore wears the same coloured clothes, I imagine, which *he* did when he was wounded . . .

I condole with Miss M. on her losses and with Eliza on her gains, and am ever yours, *J. A.*

This is Jane's first letter to survive, and was addressed to Kintbury in Berkshire where Cassandra was staying with her fiancé's family, the Fowles. By now Tom Fowle had embarked on his ill-fated mission to the West Indies as private chaplain to Lord Craven. Jane refers teasingly to a flirtation with Tom Lefroy, nephew of the Lefroys of neighbouring Ashe Rectory. It is not now possible to judge the importance of this episode to Jane, although tradition in the Lefroy family has it that Tom behaved badly to her.

'Mr. H.' was the Reverend William Heathcote, who, in spite of not knowing 'how to be particular', married Elizabeth Bigg in 1798. Alethea, who danced with James, was her sister.

STEVENTON: THURSDAY JANUARY 16 [1796]

I HAVE JUST RECEIVED YOURS and Mary's letter, and I thank you both, though their contents might have been more agreeable . . .

We are extremely sorry for poor Eliza's illness. I trust, however, that she has continued to recover since you wrote, and that you will none of you be the worse for your attendance on her . . .

Our party to Ashe tomorrow night will consist of Edward Cooper, James (for a ball is nothing without *him*), Buller, who is now staying with us, and I. I look forward with great impatience to it, as I rather expect to receive an offer from my friend in the course of the evening. I shall refuse him, however . . .

I am very much flattered by your commendation of my last letter, for I write only for fame, and without any view to pecuniary emolument . . .

Tell Mary that I make over Mr. Heartley and all his estate to her for her sole use and benefit in future, and not only him, but all my other admirers into the bargain wherever she can find them, even the kiss which C. Powlett wanted to give me, as I mean to confine myself in future to Mr. Tom Lefroy, for whom I do not care sixpence . . .

Friday. At length the day is come on which I am to flirt my last with Tom Lefroy, and when you receive this it will be over. My tears flow as I write at the melancholy idea.

I shall be extremely impatient to hear from you again, that I may know how Eliza is, and when you are to return.

With best love, etc., I am affectionately yours,

*J. A*usten

Edward Cooper was Mrs. Austen's nephew. Mr. Austen had earlier augmented his income by taking in a few pupils at Steventon Rectory, one of whom had been Buller.

ROWLING: THURSDAY 15TH SEP [1796]

My dear Cassandra

*W*E HAVE BEEN VERY gay since I wrote last; dining at Nackington, returning by moonlight, and everything quite in

BELOW *'Coming Home from a Dinner Party at Night', as depicted by Diana Sperling in 1816, a young girl who recorded her everyday impressions of Regency life. Parties were frequently planned to coincide with a full moon so as to provide illumination for the journey home.*

style, not to mention Mr. Claringbould's funeral which we saw go by on Sunday . . .

At Nackington we met Lady Sondes' picture over the mantlepiece in the dining room, and the pictures of her three children in an anteroom, besides Mr. Scott, Miss Fletcher, Mr. Toke, Mr. J. Toke, and the Archdeacon Lynch. Miss Fletcher and I were very thick, but I am the thinnest of the two. She wore her purple muslin, which is pretty enough, tho' it does not become her complexion. There are two traits in her character which are pleasing; namely, she admires Camilla, and drinks no cream in her tea . . .

We went in our two carriages to Nackington; but how we divided, I shall leave you to surmise, merely observing that as Eliz: and I were without hat or bonnet, it would not have been very convenient for us to go in the chair. We went by Bifrons, and I contemplated with a melancholy pleasure, the abode of him, on whom I once fondly doted . . .

RIGHT *Nackington House, the seat of Richard Milles Esq., a neighbour of the Knights at Godmersham. An engraving published in 1795.*

Edward and Fly went out yesterday very early in a couple of shooting jackets, and came home like a couple of bad shots, for they killed nothing at all. They are out again today, and are not yet returned. Delightful sport! They are just come home; Edward with his two brace, Frank with his two and a half. What amiable young men!

Jane was on a visit to the Edward Austens in Kent. Nackington belonged to Richard Milles, MP for Canterbury. Bifrons was the home of Edward Taylor, 'on whom I once fondly doted'.

STEVENTON : SATURDAY OCT 27 [1798]

My dear Cassandra

𝒴OUR LETTER WAS A most agreeable surprise to me today, and I have taken a long sheet of paper to show my gratitude . . .

I am very grand indeed; I had the dignity of dropping out my mother's laudanum last night. I carry about the keys of the wine and closet, and twice since I began this letter have had orders to give in the kitchen. Our dinner was very good yesterday, and the chicken boiled perfectly tender; therefore I shall not be obliged to dismiss nanny on that account.

Mrs. Hall, of Sherborne, was brought to bed yesterday of a dead child, some weeks before she expected, owing to a fright. I suppose she happened unawares to look at her husband.

We are very glad to hear such a good account of your patients, little and great. My dear itty Dordy's remembrance of me is very pleasing to me – foolishly pleasing, because I know it will be over so soon. My attachment to him will be more durable. I shall think with tenderness and delight on his beautiful and smiling countenance and interesting manners till a few years have turned him into an ungovernable, ungracious fellow . . .

ABOVE *'Shooters going out in a morning'; coloured aquatint from a drawing by Samuel Howitt.*

'Tis really very kind of my aunt to ask us to Bath again; a kindness that deserves a better return than to profit by it.

Yours ever, *J.A.*

'Dordy' was George, Edward Austen's second son, aged nearly three at this time. 'My aunt': references in the letters to 'my uncle' and 'my aunt' are always to Mr. and Mrs. Leigh Perrot. Mr. Leigh Perrot was Mrs. Austen's only brother.

SATURDAY, NOVEMBER 17 [1798]

My dear Cassandra

*I*F YOU PAID ANY ATTENTION to the conclusion of my last letter, you will be satisfied, before you receive this, that my mother has had no relapse . . .

Mrs. Lefroy did come last Wednesday . . . I was enough alone to hear all that was interesting, which you will easily credit when I tell you that of her nephew she said nothing at all, and of her friend very little. She did not once mention the name of the former to *me*, and I was too proud to make any enquiries; but on my father's afterwards asking where he was, I learnt that he was gone back to London in his way to Ireland, where he is called to the Bar and means to practise.

She showed me a letter which she had received from her friend a few weeks ago, towards the end of which was a sentence to this effect: 'I am very sorry to hear of Mrs. Austen's illness. It would give me particular pleasure to have an opportunity of improving my acquaintance with that family – with a hope of creating to myself a nearer interest. But at present I cannot indulge any expectation of it.' This is rational enough; there is less love and more sense in it than sometimes appeared before, and I am very

ABOVE *Miniature of Mrs. Lefroy. After her sudden death, Jane long remained inconsolable. 'Beloved friend, four years have passed away/Since thou wert snatched for ever from our eyes,' she wrote in her only serious poem.*

ABOVE *Little boys wore dresses until promoted, as in this illustration, to breeches. Jane was a loving aunt to her small nephews and recorded such milestones in their lives in her letters to Cassandra.*

well satisfied. It will all go on exceedingly well, and decline away in a very reasonable manner . . .

Yours, *J. A.*

Mrs. Lefroy's friend was a new suitor, the Reverend Samuel Blackall, whose pomposity did not endear him to his quarry.

Mr. Collins proposes.

❝ 'Almost as soon as I entered the house I singled you out as the companion of my future life. But before I am run away with by my feelings on this subject, perhaps it will be advisable for me to state my reasons for marrying – and moreover for coming into Hertfordshire with the design of selecting a wife, as I certainly did . . .

'My reasons for marrying are, first, that I think it a right thing for every clergyman in easy circumstances (like myself) to set the example of matrimony in his parish. Secondly, that I am convinced it will add very greatly to my happiness; and thirdly – which perhaps I ought to have mentioned earlier, that it is the particular advice and recommendation of the very noble lady whom I have the honour of calling patroness. Twice has she condescended to give me her opinion (unasked too!) on this subject; and it was but the very Saturday night before I left Hunsford – between our pools at quadrille, while Mrs. Jenkinson was arranging Miss de Bourgh's foot-stool, that she said, "Mr. Collins, you must marry. A clergyman like you must marry. Chuse properly, chuse a gentlewoman for *my* sake; and for your *own*, let her be an active, useful sort of person, not brought up high, but able to make a small income go a good way".' ❞

PRIDE AND PREJUDICE

ABOVE *'Woman churning butter.' At Steventon the Austens made butter from their own cows' milk, an important activity in a necessarily self-supporting community.*

STEVENTON: DECEMBER 1 [1798]

My dear Cassandra

I AM SO GOOD AS TO write to you again thus speedily, to let you know that I have just heard from Frank. He was at Cadiz, alive and well, on October 19, and had then very lately received a letter from you, written as long ago as when the 'London' was at St. Helen's . . .

My mother made her *entrée* into the dressing-room through crowds of admiring spectators yesterday afternoon, and we all drank tea together for the first time these five weeks. She has had a tolerable night, and bids fair for a continuance in the same brilliant course of action today . . .

Mary does not manage matters in such a way as to make me want to lay in myself. She is not tidy enough in her appearance; she has no dressing-gown to sit up in; her curtains are all too thin, and things are not in that comfort and style about her which are necessary to make such a situation an enviable one. Elizabeth was really a pretty object with her nice clean cap put on so tidily and her dress so uniformly white and orderly. We live entirely in the dressing room now . . .

We are very much disposed to like our new maid; she knows nothing of a dairy, to be sure, which, in our family, is rather against her, but she is to be taught it all. In short, we have felt the inconvenience of being without a maid so long, that we are determined to like her, and she will find it a hard matter to displease us.

Affectionately yours, *J. A.*

The dishevelled Mary was James's wife; the better arranged Elizabeth was Edward's.

THIS PAGE *'Domestic employment(s)' from W. H. Pyne's* Microcosm. *In households such as the Austens', maids had to be skilled in many departments.*

STEVENTON: TUESDAY DEC 18 [1798]

My dear Cassandra

BELOW *A fashion plate from the Gallery of Fashion for November 1798. The figure on the right is wearing a handkerchief shawl of coquelicot silk; the shade of red was the* dernier cri *of the season.*

*Y*OUR LETTER CAME QUITE as soon as I expected, and so your letters will always do, because I have made it a rule not to expect them till they come, in which I think I consult the ease of us both . . . I took the liberty a few days ago of asking your black velvet bonnet to lend me its cawl, which it very readily did, and by which I have been enabled to give a considerable improvement of dignity to my cap, which was before too *nidgetty* to please me. I shall wear it on Thursday, but I hope you will not be offended with me for following your advice as to its ornaments only in part. I still venture to retain the narrow silver round it, put twice round without any bow, and instead of the black military feather shall put in the coquelicot one, as being smarter; and besides coquelicot is to be all the fashion this winter. After the ball, I shall probably make it entirely black . . .

I have received a very civil note from Mrs. Martin requesting my name as a subscriber to her library which opens the 14th of January, and my name, or rather yours is accordingly given. My mother finds the money . . . As an inducement to subscribe Mrs. Martin tells us that her collection is not to consist only of novels, but of every kind of literature, etc. etc. She might have spared this pretension to *our* family, who are great novel-readers and not ashamed of being so . . .

We dine now at half after three, and have done dinner I suppose before you begin. We drink tea at half after six. I am afraid you will despise us. My father reads Cowper to us in the evening, to which I listen when I can. How do you spend your evenings? I guess that Elizabeth works, that you read to her, and that Edward goes to sleep. My mother continues hearty, her appetite and nights are very good, but her bowels are still not

BELOW *'The Lending Library' by Isaac Cruikshank showing the various categories of books, from the improving to the frivolous: sermons, travels, tales and romances.*

settled, and she sometimes complains of an asthma, a dropsy, water in her chest and a liver disorder . . .

Wednesday. I have changed my mind, and changed the trimmings of my cap this morning; they are now such as you suggested; I felt as if I should not prosper if I strayed from your directions, and I think it makes me look more like Lady Conyngham now than it did before, which is all that one lives for now.

J. A.

Lady Conyngham was the Prince Regent's influential mistress.

STEVENTON: MONDAY NIGHT DEC 24 [1798]

My dear Cassandra

*O*UR BALL WAS VERY thin, but by no means unpleasant. There were thirty-one people, and only eleven ladies out of the number, and but five single women in the room. Of the gentlemen present you may have some idea from the list of my partners – Mr. Wood, G. Lefroy, Rice, a Mr. Butcher (belonging to the Temples, a sailor and not of the 11th Light Dragoons), Mr. Temple (not the horrid one of all), Mr. Wm. Orde (cousin to the Kingsclere man), Mr. John Harwood, and Mr. Calland, who appeared as usual with his hat in his hand, and stood every now and then behind Catherine and me to be talked to and abused for not dancing. We teased him, however, into it at last. I was very glad to see him again after so long a separation . . .

There were twenty dances, and I danced them all, and without any fatigue . . . My black cap was openly admired by Mrs. Lefroy, and secretly I imagine by everybody else in the room . . .
Of my charities to the poor since I came home you shall have a faithful account. I have given a pair of worsted stockings to Mary

BELOW *An early nineteenth-century pen and wash drawing of a group of ladies. Jane's tiny dress allowance made the fresh trimming of last year's bonnet a matter of the greatest importance.*

Hutchins, Dame Kew, Mary Steevens, and Dame Staples; a shift to Hannah Staples, and a shawl to Betty Dawkins; amounting in all to about half a guinea . . .

I was to have dined at Deane today, but the weather is so cold that I am not sorry to be kept at home by the appearance of snow. We are to have company to dinner on Friday: the three Digweeds and James. We shall be a nice silent party, I suppose.

You deserve a longer letter than this; but it is my unhappy fate seldom to treat people so well as they deserve . . . God bless you!

Yours affectionately, *Jane Austen*

The Digweeds were the tenants of Steventon Manor. Jane's partners at the ball were neighbours, with the exception of Mr. Calland, who was probably the rector of Bentworth.

BELOW *Four girls in ball gowns from N. Heidloff's* Gallery of Fashion *for April 1800. The fashion for short hair was not always applauded by Jane: 'Anna will not be surprised that the cutting off her hair is very much regretted by several of the party in this house. I am tolerably reconciled to it by considering that two or three years may restore it again.'*

Mr. Darcy refuses to dance.

"Elizabeth Bennet had been obliged, by the scarcity of gentlemen, to sit down for two dances; and during part of that time, Mr. Darcy had been standing near enough for her to overhear a conversation between him and Mr. Bingley, who came from the dance for a few minutes, to press his friend to join in.

'Come, Darcy,' he said, 'I must have you dance. I hate to see you standing about by yourself in this stupid manner. You had much better dance.'

'I certainly shall not. You know how I detest it, unless I am particularly acquainted with my partner. At such an assembly as this, it would be insupportable . . . *You* are dancing with the only handsome girl in the room,' said Mr. Darcy, looking at the eldest Miss Bennet.

'Oh! she is the most beautiful creature I ever beheld! But there is one of her sisters sitting down just behind you, who is very pretty, and I dare say, very agreeable . . .

'Which do you mean?' and turning round, he looked for a moment at Elizabeth, till catching her eye, he withdrew his own and coldly said, 'She is tolerable; but not handsome enough to tempt *me*; and I am in no humour at present to give consequence to young ladies who are slighted by other men. You had better return to your partner and enjoy her smiles, for you are wasting your time with me.'

Mr. Bingley followed his advice. Mr. Darcy walked off; and Elizabeth remained with no very cordial feelings towards him. She told the story however with great spirit among her friends; for she had a lively, playful disposition, which delighted in anything ridiculous. **"**

PRIDE AND PREJUDICE

STEVENTON : FRIDAY DEC 28 [1798]

My dear Cassandra

*F*RANK IS MADE. He was yesterday raised to the rank of Commander and appointed to the Petterel sloop, now at Gibraltar. As soon as you have cried a little for joy, you may go on, and learn farther that the India House have taken *Captn Austen's* petition into consideration – this comes from Daysh – and likewise that Lieut: Charles John Austen is removed to the *Tamar* frigate – this comes from the Admiral. We cannot find out where the Tamar is, but I hope we shall now see Charles here at all events.

This letter is to be dedicated entirely to good news. If you will send my father an account of your washing and letter expenses etc., he will send you a draft for the amount of it, as well as for your next quarter, and for Edward's rent. If you don't buy a

ABOVE *Miniature of Francis (Frank) Austen, the elder of Jane's two distinguished sailor brothers, with whom she had an easy relationship. 'I hope you continue beautiful and brush your hair, but not all off,' she wrote.*

muslin gown now on the strength of this money, and Frank's promotion, I shall never forgive you.

Mrs. Lefroy has just sent me word that Lady Dorchester means to invite me to her ball on the 8th of January, which tho' an humble blessing compared with what the last page records, I do not consider as any calamity. I cannot write any more now, but I have written enough to make you very happy, and therefore may safely conclude.

Yours affecly *Jane*

Lady Dorchester, of Kempshott Park, Hampshire.

STEVENTON: TUESDAY JANRY 8 [1799]

My dear Cassandra

*Y*OU MUST READ YOUR letters over *five* times in future before you send them, and then, perhaps, you may find them as entertaining as I do. I laughed at several parts of the one which I am now answering . . .

You express so little anxiety about my being murdered under Ashe Park Copse by Mrs. Hulbert's servant, that I have a great mind not to tell you whether I was or not, and shall only say that I did not return home that night or the next, as Martha kindly made room for me in her bed, which was the shut-up one in the new nursery. Nurse and the child slept upon the floor, and there we all were in some confusion and great comfort. The bed did exceedingly well for us, both to lie awake in and talk till two o'clock, and to sleep in the rest of the night. I love Martha better than ever, and I mean to go and see her, if I can, when she gets home . . .

I am tolerably glad to hear that Edward's income is so good a one . . .

ABOVE *A muslin dress of January 1796. Sprigged or spotted muslin was much in demand. Jane coveted and bought a 'pretty coloured muslin . . . with a small red spot' to make dresses for herself and Cassandra.*

RIGHT *Portrait of Edward Austen Knight. The classical relief probably alluded to his Grand Tour, often undertaken by the sons of the landed gentry and aristocracy.*

Mrs. Knight giving up the Godmersham estate to Edward was no such prodigious act of generosity after all, it seems, for she has reserved herself an income out of it still; this ought to be known, that her conduct may not be overrated. I rather think Edward shows the most magnanimity of the two, in accepting her resignation with such incumbrances . . .

I spent a very pleasant evening, chiefly among the Manydown party. There was the same kind of supper as last year, and the same want of chairs. There were more dancers than the room could conveniently hold, which is enough to constitute a good ball at any time.

I do not think I was very much in request. People were rather apt not to ask me till they could not help it; one's consequence, you know, varies so much at times without any particular reason. There was one gentleman, an officer of the Cheshire, a very good-looking young man, who, I was told, wanted very much to be introduced to me; but as he did not want it quite enough to take much trouble in effecting it, we never could bring it about . . .

I do not wonder at your wanting to read 'First Impressions' again, so seldom as you have gone through it, and that so long ago . . .

I *shall* be able to send this to the post today, which exalts me to the utmost pinnacle of human felicity, and makes me bask in the sunshine of prosperity, or gives me any other sensation of pleasure in studied language which you may prefer. Do not be angry with me for not filling my sheet . . .

Yours affectionately, *J. A.*

Martha Lloyd was the sister of Mary, Mrs. James Austen. Mrs. Knight reserved a £2000 annuity on resigning the Godmersham estate to Edward. This letter contains the first reference to the novel that would become Pride and Prejudice.

ABOVE *Godmersham, the home of Edward Austen Knight and his large family, engraved for J. P. Neale's* Views of the Seats of Noblemen and Gentlemen, *1826.*

13 QUEEN SQUARE – SUNDAY JUNE 2 [1799]

My dear Cassandra

I AM OBLIGED TO YOU for two letters, one from yourself and the other from Mary, for of the latter I knew nothing till on the receipt of yours yesterday, when the pigeon basket was examined and I received my due . . .

What must I tell you of Edward? Truth or falsehood? I will try the former, and you may chuse for yourself another time. He was better yesterday than he had been for two or three days before, about as well as while he was at Steventon. He drinks at the Hetling pump, is to bathe tomorrow, and try electricity on Tuesday; he proposed the latter himself to Dr. Fellowes, who made no objection to it, but I fancy we are all unanimous in expecting no advantage from it . . .

I saw some gauzes in a shop in Bath Street yesterday at only 4s. a yard, but they were not so good or so pretty as mine. Flowers are very much worn, and fruit is still more the thing. Eliz: has a bunch of strawberries, and I have seen grapes, cherries, plums and apricots. There are likewise, almonds and raisins, French plums and tamarinds at the grocers, but I have never seen any of them in hats . . .

We took a very charming walk from 6 to 8 up Beacon Hill, and across some fields to the village of Charlcombe, which is sweetly situated in a little green valley, as a village with such a name ought to be . . . We had a Miss North and a Mr. Gould of our party; the latter walked home with me after tea; he is a very young man, just entered of Oxford, wears spectacles, and has heard that Evelina was written by Dr. Johnson . . .

There is to be a grand gala on Tuesday evening in Sydney Gardens; a concert, with illuminations and fireworks; to the latter Eliz: and I look forward with pleasure, and even the concert

ABOVE *Sketch of King's Bath and Pump Room, with Bath Abbey in the distance.*

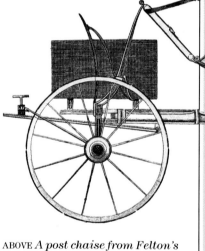

ABOVE *A post chaise from Felton's Treatise on Carriages, 1794. He wrote, 'families who often journey from place to place with post horses, do well to furnish themselves with a post chaise'. The added luxury would however have to be weighed against the considerable outlay.*

will have more than its usual charm with me, as the gardens are large enough for me to get pretty well beyond the reach of its sound . . .

I am quite pleased with Martha and Mrs. Lefroy for wanting the pattern of our caps, but I am not so well pleased with your giving it to them. Some wish, some prevailing wish is necessary to the animation of everybody's mind, and in gratifying this, you leave them to form some other which will not probably be half so innocent. I shall not forget to write to Frank. Duty and love etc.

Yours affecly ane

Jane wrote this letter from Bath, where she and Mrs. Austen were staying with Edward and Elizabeth Austen. Edward was undergoing various treatments in an attempt to ward off incipient gout.

STEVENTON SATURDAY EVENG – NOVR 8 [1800]

My dear Cassandra,

ℋAVING JUST FINISHED THE first volume of Les Veillées du Château, I think it a good opportunity for beginning a letter to you while my mind is stored with ideas worth transmitting . . .

I cannot possibly oblige you by not wearing my gown, because I have it made up on purpose to wear it a great deal, and as the discredit will be my own, I feel the less regret. You must learn to like it yourself and make it up at Godmersham; it may easily be done; it is only protesting it to be very beautiful, and you will soon think it so. Yesterday was a day of great business with me; Mary drove me all in the rain to Basingstoke, and still more all in the rain back again, because it rained harder; and soon after our return to Dean a sudden invitation and an own postchaise took

ABOVE *Sketch of Charlcombe Church. Jane had taken 'a very charming walk . . . across some fields to the village of Charlcombe, which is sweetly situated in a little green valley, as a village with such a name ought to be'.*

us to Ashe Park, to dine tête à tête with Mr. Holder, Mr. Gauntlett and James Digweed; but our tête à tête was cruelly reduced by the non-attendance of the two latter. Sometimes we talked and sometimes we were quite silent; I said two or three amusing things . . .

am yrs ever *J.A.*

Sunday Evening. We have had a dreadful storm of wind in the forepart of this day, which has done a great deal of mischief among our trees. I was sitting alone in the dining room, when an odd kind of crash startled me – in a moment afterwards it was repeated; I then went to the window, which I reached just in time to see the last of our two highly valued elms descend into the sweep ! ! ! ! !

This is not all. One large elm out of two on the left hand side, as you enter what I call the elm walk, was likewise blown down, the maypole bearing the weathercock was broke in two, and what I regret more than all the rest, is that all the three elms which grew in Hall's meadow and gave such ornament to it, are gone . . .

I hope it is true that Edward Taylor is to marry his cousin Charlotte. Those beautiful dark eyes will then adorn another generation at least in all their purity.

To Martha Lloyd

STEVENTON WEDNESDAY EVENG. NOVR 12 [1800]

My dear Martha

I DID NOT RECEIVE YOUR note yesterday till after Charlotte had left Deane, or I would have sent my answer by her, instead of being the means, as I now must be, of lessening the elegance of your new dress for the Hurstbourne Ball by the value of 3d . . .

LEFT *Pattern for a dancing dress published in Ackermann's Repository, February 1809. 'I wish such things were to be bought ready-made,' Jane complained. 'I want to have something suggested which will give me no trouble of thought or direction.'*

You distress me cruelly by your request about books; I cannot think of any to bring with me, nor have I any idea of our wanting them. I come to you to be talked to, not to read or hear reading. I can do *that* at home; and indeed I am now laying in a stock of intelligence to pour out on you as *my* share of conversation. I am reading Henry's History of England, which I will repeat to you in any manner you may prefer, either in a loose, desultory, unconnected strain, or dividing my recital as the historian divides it himself, into seven parts, The Civil and Military – Religion – Constitution – Learning and Learned Men – Arts and Sciences – Commerce Coins and Shipping – and Manners; so that for every evening of the week there will be a different subject; the Friday's lot, Commerce, Coin and Shipping, you will find the least entertaining; but the next eveng:'s portion will make amends. We all unite in best love, and I am

Yr very affecte *J.A.*

STEVENTON THURSDAY NOVR 20 [1800]

My dear Cassandra

*Y*OUR LETTER TOOK ME quite by surprise this morning; you are very welcome however, and I am very much obliged to you. I believe I drank too much wine last night at Hurstbourne; I know not how else to account for the shaking of my hand today; you will kindly make allowance therefore for any indistinctness of writing by attributing it to this venial error . . .

It was a pleasant evening, Charles found it remarkably so, but I cannot tell why, unless the absence of Miss Terry – towards whom his conscience reproaches him with now being perfect indifferent – was a relief to him. There were only twelve dances, of which I danced nine, and was merely prevented from dancing

the rest by the want of a partner . . . There were very few beauties, and such as there were, were not very handsome. Miss Iremonger did not look well, and Mrs. Blount was the only one much admired. She appeared exactly as she did in September, with the same broad face, diamond bandeau, white shoes, pink husband, and fat neck . . .

We had a very pleasant day on Monday at Ashe; we sat down 14 to dinner in the study, the dining room being not habitable from the storm's having blown down its chimney. Mrs. Bramston talked a good deal of nonsense, which Mr. Bramston and Mr. Clerk seemed almost equally to enjoy. There was a whist and a casino table, and six outsiders. Rice and Lucy made love, Mat: Robinson fell asleep, James and Mrs. Augusta alternately read Dr. Jenner's pamphlet on the cow pox, and I bestowed my company by turns on all . . .

The three Digweeds all came on Tuesday, and we played a pool at commerce. James Digweed left Hampshire today. I think he must be in love with you, from his anxiety to have you go to the Faversham Balls, and likewise from his supposing that the two elms fell from their grief at your absence. Was not it a gallant idea? . . .

Farewell. Charles sends you his best love and Edward his worst. If you think the distinction improper, you may take the worst yourself. He will write to you when he gets back to his ship – and in the meantime desires that you will consider me as

Your affec: sister *J.A.*

Charles likes my gown now.

Mrs. Augusta Bramston. She found Sense and Sensibility *and* Pride and Prejudice *'downright nonsense, but expected to like* Mansfield Park *better, and having finished the first volume flattered herself she had got through the worst'.*

BELOW *'House Maid' from Pyne's World in Miniature. 'John Steevens' wife undertakes our purification. She does not look as if anything she touched would ever be clean.'*

BELOW *'House Maid' from Pyne's World in Miniature. 'John Steevens' wife undertakes our purification. She does not look as if anything she touched would ever be clean.'*

STEVENTON: SATURDAY JANRY 3d [1801]

My dear Cassandra

*A*S YOU HAVE BY this time received my last letter, it is fit that I should begin another . . .

My mother looks forward with as much certainty as you can do, to our keeping two maids — my father is the only one not in the secret. We plan having a steady cook, and a young giddy house-maid, with a sedate, middle-aged man, who is to undertake the double office of husband to the former and sweetheart to the latter. No children of course to be allowed on either side . . .

I have now attained the true art of letter-writing, which we are always told, is to express on paper exactly what one would say to the same person by word of mouth; I have been talking to you almost as fast as I could the whole of this letter . . .

My mother bargains for having no trouble at all in furnishing our house in Bath — and I have engaged for your willingly undertaking to do it all. I get more and more reconciled to the idea of our removal. We have lived long enough in this neigh-bourhood, the Basingstoke Balls are certainly on the decline, there is something interesting in the bustle of going away, and the prospect of spending future summers by the sea or in Wales is very delightful . . . It must not be generally known however that I am not sacrificing a great deal in quitting the country – or I can expect to inspire no tenderness, no interest in those we leave behind.

My father is doing all in his power to increase his income by raising his tithes etc., and I do not despair of getting very nearly six hundred a year. In what part of Bath do you mean to place your *bees*? We are afraid of the South Parade's being too hot . . .

Yours affectly *J. A.*

BELOW *A view of Pulteney Street, terminating in Laura Place, as seen through the gateway going out of Sydney Gardens. 'The houses in the streets near Laura Place I should expect to be above our price,' wrote Jane.*

BATH 1801–1805

• ● •

Farewells
and Uncertainties

LEFT *A general view of Bath from the Claverton Road from John Claude Nattes' Bath. He writes, 'The spot from which this drawing was made is in the parish of Widcombe.' Jane Austen would have seen this view as she walked over the hills with energetic Mrs. Chamberlayne on 21 May 1801.*

A few of Jane's letters survive from May 1801, at which time she and Mrs. Austen were already in Bath, staying with the Leigh Perrots in No. 1 Paragon while searching for a suitable house. At the end of the month they rented 4 Sydney Terrace, at that time still overlooking pleasant open country on the city's outskirts, where they were joined by Mr. Austen and Cassandra.

A long gap in the correspondence follows: one solitary letter from Lyme Regis in September 1804; then a further silence until the end of June 1805. For this period it is only possible to reconstruct the family's movements from hints and glimpses. They spent long holidays in the West Country, at Sidmouth, Dawlish, Teignmouth and Lyme Regis. On one occasion the mildness of the western climate permitted a visit to Lyme as late as November (as it would also for the Musgroves in *Persuasion*). These major expeditions were interspersed with visits to Steventon (where James was now installed as rector), to Godmersham and elsewhere.

It was at some point during these years that Jane experienced what was probably the only serious romance of her life. In her memoir of her Aunt Jane, Caroline tells of Cassandra many years later confiding that one summer, when she and Jane were by the sea, they met a gentleman who 'seemed greatly attracted by my Aunt Jane . . . I can only say that the impression left on Aunt Cassandra was that he had fallen in love with her sister, and was

RIGHT *A view of Dawlish from the West Cliff, taken from W. B. Noble's* A Guide to Watering Places, *1817. Jane enjoyed escaping from the oppressions of Bath to spend holidays at one of the West Country resorts.*

quite in earnest. Soon afterwards they heard of his death.' This sorrow, combined with the absence of a settled home, might well help to explain the apparent cessation of her literary activity. Sometime during the winter of 1802–3, however, she may have revised *Susan*; and she certainly sold the manuscript to a publisher, Crosby, for ten pounds. He never used it.

At the end of November 1802 the Austen sisters began a visit, planned to last for several weeks, to their old friends Catherine and Alethea Bigg at Manydown, near Steventon. But after only a few days all four girls arrived in tears at Steventon Rectory, Cassandra and Jane refusing to explain themselves, but insisting that their brother James should take them back to Bath immediately, abandoning his Sunday duties. It later transpired that Harris Bigg Wither, the son of the house, had proposed to Jane and been accepted; but by the next morning she had changed her mind. Perhaps the contrast with her dead love was too much to bear; or perhaps the temptation of what amounted to a most desirable match, both from a worldly point of view and also from

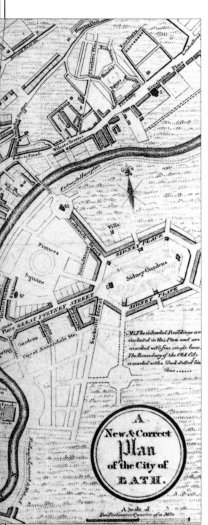

the promised joy of a return to her friends and to the Steventon neighbourhood, proved insufficient when set against the prospect of a loveless marriage.

On Jane's twenty-ninth birthday, 16 December 1804, her dear friend, Mrs Lefroy, was killed in a fall from her horse. Still shattered from this blow, Jane had to write to Frank in January 1805 to announce Mr. Austen's death after a brief illness.

Mrs. Austen found herself left with a disconcertingly reduced income, but her sons between them contributed a sufficient sum to allow her a modest competence, with which she was perfectly content. Cassandra had a small legacy left her by Tom Fowle, but Jane possessed nothing. This dependence on her brothers' charity helps to underline the desirability of an escape into marriage for a spinster of her time and class, and sets her rejection of Harris Bigg Wither in a sharper focus. The close and loving bond between all the Austen children, however, made her plight less painful than it might otherwise have been.

In March 1805 Mrs. Austen took lodgings in 25 Gay Street, and shortly afterwards Cassandra went to Ibthorpe to help Martha Lloyd nurse her mother. Mrs. Lloyd died in April, leaving Martha with a lonely prospect; but an invitation to make her home with the Austen ladies was gladly accepted, and proved a happy arrangement, lasting until after Mrs. Austen's death in 1827.

Frank Austen, meanwhile, suffered the disappointment in October 1805 of being sent on a minor mission which resulted in his narrowly missing the Battle of Trafalgar. By the next year he had amassed enough prize money to allow him to marry his fiancée, Mary Gibson. It was decided that he and his bride should set up house in Southampton with his mother, sisters and Martha; and on 2 July 1805 the Austen party left Bath with no regrets, but, as Jane wrote later, with 'happy feelings of escape'.

Jane's equable temperament, combined with an entranced absorption in the minutiae of life, must have helped to carry her through this somewhat grey time. Nothing that passed before

LEFT *'A New and Correct Plan of the City of Bath' from* The Original Bath Guide, *1811, showing the confines of the city in Jane Austen's day.*

that thoughtful gaze was wasted. The adulteress noted in her letter of 12 May 1801; cross Mr. Evelyn, who must be harmless because 'he gets groundsel for his birds and all that'; the happy reception of Charles's gift to his sisters of topaz crosses (later immortalized in the episode of Fanny's amber cross in *Mansfield Park*); the gentle tact of her letter breaking the news to Frank of his father's death; all these share a characteristic: that magic touch transforming the commonplace into the very stuff of art.

PARAGON – TUESDAY MAY 5 [1801]

My dear Cassandra

I HAVE THE PLEASURE OF writing from my *own* room up two pair of stairs, with everything very comfortable about me . . .

I have given the soap and the baskets, and each have been kindly received. *One* thing only among all our concerns has not arrived in safety; when I got into the chaise at Devizes I discovered that your drawing ruler was broke in two; it is just at the top where the cross-piece is fastened on. I beg pardon.

There is to be only one more ball – next Monday is the day. The Chamberlaynes are still here; I begin to think better of Mrs. C—, and upon recollection believe she has rather a long chin than otherwise, as she remembers us in Gloucestershire when we were very charming young women.

The first view of Bath in fine weather does not answer my expectations; I think I see more distinctly thro' rain. The sun was behind everything, and the appearance of the place from the top of Kingsdown was all vapour, shadow, smoke, and confusion . . .

Tuesday night. When my uncle went to take his second glass of water I walked with him, and in our morning's circuit we looked at two houses in Green Park Buildings, one of which pleased me very well . . .

ABOVE *'Waterman to a coach stand', from Pyne's* Costume of Great Britain: *'His business is to feed and water horses, and to open the door for passengers, that the driver may remain upon his box . . . he also has charge of the coaches during the time the coachmen take their meals.' Journeys involved all the petty irritations incumbent upon the frequent stops to change horses.*

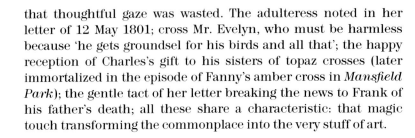

ABOVE *Walking Dress from* La Belle Assemblée *for July to December 1809: a white muslin dress with a spenser bodice of pale pink sarsnet over which is a black gauze mantle and train, an Egyptian bonnet of pink sarsnet and antique lace.*

Wednesday ... My mother has ordered a new bonnet, and so have I; both white strip, trimmed with white ribbon. I find my straw bonnet looking very much like other people's and quite as smart. Bonnets of cambric muslin on the plan of Lady Bridges' are a good deal worn, and some of them are very pretty; but I shall defer one of that sort till your arrival. Bath is getting so very empty that I am not afraid of doing too little. Black gauze cloaks are worn as much as anything. I shall write again in a day or two. Best love.

Yrs ever *J.A.*

Mrs. Chamberlayne of Maugersbury House, Gloucestershire, was a neighbour of Jane Austen's cousins, the Thomas Leighs of Adlestrop Rectory. Mr. Leigh Perrot was taking a course of the Bath waters as a cure for gout and Jane accompanied him when he took his 'second glass of water'.

ABOVE AND FAR RIGHT *Silhouettes of Mr. and Mrs. Leigh Perrot, Jane Austen's aunt and uncle. The Austen daughters visited their uncle, Mrs. Austen's brother, and his wife at their fine town house, No. 1 Paragon.*

RIGHT *South Parade, Bath, a late eighteenth-century watercolour by Thomas Malton. 'In what part of Bath do you mean to place your bees? We are afraid of the South Parade's being too hot,' Jane teased Cassandra.*

PARAGON – TUESDAY MAY 12 [1801]

My dear Cassandra

ABOVE AND RIGHT *Scenes from a cattle market. At over twenty pounds a head, Mr. Austen could feel himself fortunate in the sale of his cows on leaving Steventon.*

MY MOTHER HAS HEARD from Mary and I have heard from Frank; we therefore know something now of our concerns in distant quarters, and you I hope by some means or other are equally instructed . . . James I dare say has been over to Ibthorpe by this time to enquire particularly after Mrs. Lloyd's health, and forestall whatever intelligence of the sale I might attempt to give. Sixty one guineas and a half for the three cows gives one some support under the blow of only eleven guineas for the tables. Eight for my pianoforte is about what I really expected to get; I am more anxious to know the amount of my books, especially as they are said to have sold well . . .

We met not a creature at Mrs. Lillingstone's, and yet were not so very stupid as I expected, which I attribute to my wearing my new bonnet and being in good looks . . .

In the evening I hope you honoured my toilette and ball with a thought; I dressed myself as well as I could, and had all my finery much admired at home. By nine o'clock my uncle, aunt and I entered the rooms and linked Miss Winstone on to us. Before tea it was rather a dull affair; but then the before tea did not last long, for there was only one dance, danced by four couple. Think of four couple, surrounded by about an hundred people, dancing in the Upper Rooms at Bath!

After tea we *cheered up*; the breaking up of private parties sent some scores more to the ball, and tho' it was shockingly and inhumanly thin for this place, there were people enough to have made five or six very pretty Basingstoke assemblies . . .

I am proud to say that I have a very good eye at an adulteress, for tho' repeatedly assured that another in the same party was the *she*, I fixed upon the right one from the first. A resemblance to

Mrs. L. was my guide. She is not so pretty as I expected . . . she was highly rouged, and looked rather quietly and contentedly silly than anything else . . .

Wednesday. Another stupid party last night; perhaps if larger they might be less intolerable, but here there were only just enough to make one card table, with six people to look on and talk nonsense to each other. Lady Fust, Mrs. Busby and a Mrs. Owen sat down with my uncle to whist, within five minutes after the three old toughs came in, and there they sat . . . till their chairs were announced.

I cannot anyhow continue to find people agreeable; I respect Mrs. Chamberlayne for doing her hair well, but cannot feel a more tender sentiment. Miss Langley is like any other short girl, with a broad nose and wide mouth, fashionable dress and exposed bosom. Adm: Stanhope is a gentlemanlike man, but then his legs are too short, and his tail too long . . .

Yrs ever *J. A.*

ABOVE *New Assembly Rooms, commonly called the Upper Rooms in contradistinction to the Old Assembly Rooms which were in the Lower Town by the North Parade. The New Assembly Rooms remain resplendent to this day.*

The 'adulteress' was the Hon. Mrs. Edward Ricketts, who was divorced for adultery with Captain Richard Graves. The romance sent ripples of glee through Hampshire society.

PARAGON – THURSDAY MAY 21 [1801]

My dear Cassandra

*T*O MAKE LONG SENTENCES upon unpleasant subjects is very odious, and I shall therefore get rid of the one now uppermost in my thoughts as soon as possible.

Our views on G. P. Buildings seem all at an end; the observation of the damps still remaining in the offices of an house which has been only vacated a week, with reports of discontented

ABOVE *Axford and Paragon Buildings, Bath. 'We know,' wrote Jane to Cassandra, 'that Mrs. Perrot will want to get us in Axford Buildings, but we all unite in particular dislike of that part of the town, and therefore hope to escape.'*

families and putrid fevers, has given the coup de grâce. We have now nothing in view . . .

The friendship between Mrs. Chamberlayne and me which you predicted has already taken place, for we shake hands whenever we meet. Our grand walk to Weston was again fixed for yesterday, and was accomplished in a very striking manner. Every one of the party declined it under some pretence or other except our two selves, and we had therefore a tête à tête but *that* we should equally have had after the first two yards had half the inhabitants of Bath set off with us.

It would have amused you to see our progress; we went up by Sion Hill, and returned across the fields; in climbing a hill Mrs. Chamberlayne is very capital; I could with difficulty keep pace with her, yet would not flinch for the world. On plain ground I was quite her equal. And so we posted away under a fine hot sun, *she* without any parasol or any shade to her hat, stopping for nothing, and crossing the churchyard at Weston with as much expedition as if we were afraid of being buried alive. After seeing what she is equal to, I cannot help feeling a regard for her . . .

We are to have a tiny party here tonight. I hate tiny parties, they force one into constant exertion. Miss Edwards and her father, Mrs. Busby and her nephew, Mr. Maitland, and Mrs. Lillingstone are to be the whole; and I am prevented from setting my black cap at Mr. Maitland by his having a wife and ten children . . .

You will be sorry to hear that Marianne Mapleton's disorder has ended fatally. She was believed out of danger on Sunday, but a sudden relapse carried her off the next day. So affectionate a family must suffer severely; and many a girl on early death has been praised into an angel I believe, on slighter pretensions to beauty, sense and merit than Marianne.

Mr. Bent seems *bent* upon being very detestable, for he values the books at only £70. The whole world is in a conspiracy to enrich one part of our family at the expense of another. Ten

ABOVE *An engraving of Green Park Buildings, Bath. The family were living at No. 27 at the time of Mr. Austen's death.*

shillings for Dodsley's Poems however please me to the quick, and I do not care how often I sell them for as much . . .

Yrs ever *J. A.*

Marianne was the daughter of Dr. Mapleton of Bath. Robert Dodsley wrote several poems while working as a footman, including The Muse in Livery. *Later he became a bookseller, suggested to Dr. Johnson the idea of compiling a dictionary, and, with Burke, founded the* Annual Register.

PARAGON – TUESDAY MAY 26 [1801]

My dear Cassandra

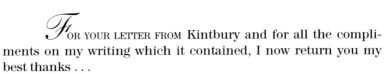

FOR YOUR LETTER FROM Kintbury and for all the compliments on my writing which it contained, I now return you my best thanks . . .

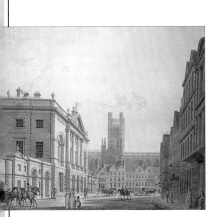

ABOVE *Watercolour view of the High Street Bath, c.1777, by Thomas Malton.*

The Endymion came into Portsmouth on Sunday, and I have sent Charles a short letter by this day's post. My adventures since I wrote you three days ago have been such as the time would easily contain; I walked yesterday morning with Mrs. Chamberlayne to Lyncombe and Widcombe, and in the evening I drank tea with the Holders. Mrs. Chamberlayne's pace was not quite so magnificent on this second trial as on the first; it was nothing more than I could keep up with, without effort; and for many, many yards together on a raised narrow footpath I led the way. The walk was very beautiful as my companion agreed whenever I made the observation. And so ends our friendship, for the Chamberlaynes leave Bath in a day or two . . .

My evening visit was by no means disagreeable. Mrs. Lillingston came to engage Mrs. Holder's conversation, and Miss Holder and I adjourned after tea to the inner drawing room to look over

ABOVE *Watercolour of Pulteney Bridge by Thomas Malton, 1785.*

prints and talk pathetically. She is very unreserved and very fond of talking of her deceased brother and sister, whose memories she cherishes with an enthusiasm which, tho' perhaps a little affected, is not unpleasing. She has an idea of your being remarkably lively; therefore get ready the proper selection of adverbs, and due scraps of Italian and French . . .

I assure you in spite of what I might chuse to insinuate in a former letter, that I have seen very little of Mr. Evelyn since my coming here; I met him this morning for only the 4th time . . . I made the most of the story . . . but in fact he only asked me whether I were to be in Sydney Gardens in the evening or not. There is now something like an engagement between us and the phaeton, which to confess my frailty I have a great desire to go out in; whether it will come to anything must remain with him. I really believe he is very harmless; people do not seem afraid of him here, and he gets groundsel for his birds and all that . . .

Yrs affect:ly

Wednesday. I am just returned from my airing in the very bewitching phaeton and four for which I was prepared by a note from Mr. E. soon after breakfast: we went to the top of Kingsdown, and had a very pleasant drive . . . On my return I found your letter and a letter from Charles on the table . . . He has received £30 for his share of the privateer and expects £10 more, but of what avail is it to take prizes if he lays out the produce in presents to his sisters? He has been buying gold chains and topaz crosses for us; he must be well scolded . . . He will receive my yesterday's letter today, and I shall write again by this post to thank and reproach him. We shall be unbearably fine.

William Evelyn of St. Clere, Kent, was a friend of Edward's. As Lieutenant on the Endymion, *Charles was entitled to a share in the prize money, in this instance from the capture of* La Furie.

ABOVE *A pen and wash view of Kingsdown. It was from this viewpoint that Jane described her arrival in Bath, coloured by the sadness of leaving Steventon. 'The sun was got behind everything, and the appearance of the place from the top of Kingsdown was all vapour, shadow, smoke, and confusion.'*

ABOVE *A phaeton from* A Treatise on Carriages *by the coachmaker William Felton, who wrote of it: 'The expense for building such a carriage in the superior manner, and furnishing with convenience is very great, and nearly on a par with the chariot . . . great care should be observed in turning short, lest by the height of the body and weight of the passengers it should overpoise, which is the only danger to be apprehended from them; on every other account they are to be preferred.'*

"A very short trial convinced her that a curricle was the prettiest equipage in the world . . . But the merit of the curricle did not all belong to the horses; Henry drove so well, — so quietly — without making any disturbance, without parading to her, or swearing at them; so different from the only gentleman-coachman whom it was in her power to compare him with! And then his hat sat so well, and the innumerable capes of his great coat looked so becomingly important! To be driven by him, next to being dancing with him, was certainly the greatest happiness in the world."

NORTHANGER ABBEY

Catherine Morland discovers the pleasures of being driven by Heny Tilney.

"To her, the cares were sometimes almost beyond the happiness; for young and inexperienced, with small means of choice and no confidence in her own taste — the 'how she should be dressed' was a point of painful solicitude; and the almost solitary ornament in her possession, a very pretty amber cross which William had brought her from Sicily, was the greatest distress of all, for she had nothing but a bit of ribbon to fasten it to; and though she had worn it in that manner once, would it be allowable at such a time, in the midst of all the rich ornaments which she supposed all the other young ladies would appear in? And yet not to wear it! William had wanted to buy her a gold chain too, but the purchase had been beyond his means, and therefore not to wear the cross might be mortifying him. These were anxious considerations; enough to sober her spirits even under the prospect of a ball given principally for her gratification."

MANSFIELD PARK

Fanny Price agonises over the preparations for her first ball.

LYME, FRIDAY SEPT. 14 [1804]

My dear Cassandra

BELOW AND RIGHT *Details from Thomas Wilson's* Correct Method of German and French Waltzing.

I TAKE THE FIRST SHEET of this fine striped paper to thank you for your letter from Weymouth, and express my hopes of your being at Ibthorpe before this time . . .

You found my letter at Andover I hope yesterday, and have now for many hours been satisfied that your kind anxiety on my behalf was as much thrown away as kind anxiety usually is. I continue quite well in proof of which I have bathed again this morning. It was absolutely necessary that I should have the little fever and indisposition which I had; it has been all the fashion this week in Lyme . . .

We are quite settled in our lodgings by this time, as you may suppose, and everything goes on in the usual order. The servants behave very well, and make no difficulties, tho' nothing certainly can exceed the inconvenience of the offices, except the general dirtiness of the house and furniture, and all its inhabitants . . . I endeavour . . . to supply your place, and be useful and keep things in order. I detect dirt in the water decanter as fast as I can, and give the cook physic, which she throws off her stomach. I forget whether she used to do this, under your administration . . .

The ball last night was pleasant, but not full for Thursday. My father stayed very contentedly till half-past nine – we went a little after eight – and then walked home with James and a lanthorn, tho' I believe the lanthorn was not lit, as the moon was up. But this lanthorn may sometimes be a great convenience to him. My mother and I stayed about an hour later. Nobody asked me the two first dances – the two next I danced with Mr. Crawford – and had I chosen to stay longer might have danced with Mr. Granville, Mrs. Granville's son – whom my dear friend Miss Armstrong introduced to me – or with a new, odd-looking man, who had

RIGHT *The Cloakroom of the Clifton Assembly Rooms, a painting by Rolina Sharples. Jane and her family would have made part of many such a scene in Bath. (The lady in the foreground is helped by a maid to change her shoes and on the left on officer in the Dragoons bows to an acquaintance.)*

been eyeing me for some time, and at last without any introduction asked me if I meant to dance again. I think he must be Irish by his ease, and because I imagine him to belong to the Hon.ble Barnwalls, who are the son and son's wife of an Irish viscount — bold queer-looking people, just fit to be quality at Lyme . . .

I called yesterday morning (ought it not in strict propriety to be termed yester-morning?) on Miss Armstrong and was introduced to her father and mother. Like other young ladies she is considerably genteeler than her parents. Mrs. Armstrong sat darning a pair of stockings the whole of my visit. But I do not mention this at home, lest a warning should act as an example. We afterwards walked together for an hour on the Cobb; she is very conversable in a common way; I do not perceive wit or genius, but she has sense and some degree of taste, and her manners are very engaging. She seems to like people rather too easily . . .

I need not say that we are particularly anxious for your next letter to know how you find Mrs. Lloyd and Martha.

Yrs affecly *J.A.*

Mrs. Austen was apt to continue darning in the presence of visitors, hence Jane's caution not to mention to their mother that Mrs. Armstrong had done so, 'lest a warning should act as an example'.

ABOVE *John Nixon's drawing of his wife and friend busy at their sewing: a typical domestic interior of the time.*

BELOW *Jane Austen's Lyme Regis: an aquatint of the early nineteenth century. Jane extolled Lyme Regis in* Persuasion, *'Its old wonders and new improvements, with the very beautiful line of cliffs stretching out to the east of the town are what the stranger's eye will seek; and a very strange stranger it must be, who does not see charms in the immediate environment of Lyme, to make him wish to know it better.'*

"There was too much wind to make the high part of the new Cobb pleasant for the ladies, and they agreed to get down the steps to the lower, and all were contented to pass quietly and carefully down the steep flight, excepting Louisa; she must be jumped down them by Captain Wentworth. In all their walks, he had had to jump her from the styles; the sensation was delightful to her. The hardness of the pavement for her feet, made him less willing upon the present occasion; he did it, however; she was safely down, and instantly, to shew her enjoyment, ran up the steps to be jumped down again. He advised her against it, thought the jar too great; but no, he reasoned and talked in vain; she smiled and said, 'I am determined I will:' he put out his hands; she was too precipitate by half a second, she fell on the pavement on the Lower Cobb, and was taken up lifeless!"

PERSUASION

Louisa Musgrove's fall from the Cobb at Lyme Regis.

To Captain Francis Austen

GREEN PARK BGS. TUESDAY EVENG, JANRY 22 [1805]

My dearest Frank

I WROTE TO YOU YESTERDAY; but your letter to Cassandra this morning, by which we learn the probability of your being by this time at Portsmouth, obliges me to write to you again, having, unfortunately, a communication as necessary as painful to make to you. Your affectionate heart will be greatly wounded, and I wish the shock could have been lessened . . . but the event has been sudden, and so must be the information of it.

We have lost our excellent father. An illness of only eight and forty hours carried him off yesterday morning . . .

Everything I trust and believe was done for him that was possible. It has been very sudden! Within twenty-four hours of his death he was walking with only the help of a stick, was even reading! We had however some hours of preparation, and when we understood his recovery to be hopeless, most fervently did we pray for the speedy release which ensued. To have seen him languishing long, struggling for hours, would have been dreadful! and thank God! we were all spared from it. Except the restlessness and confusion of high fever, he did not suffer and he was mercifully spared from knowing that he was about to quit objects so beloved, and so . . . cherished as his wife and children ever were.

His tenderness as a father, who can do justice to? My mother is tolerably well; she bears up with the greatest fortitude, but I fear her health must suffer under such a shock. An express was sent for James, and he arrived here this morning before eight o'clock.

The funeral is to be on Saturday at Walcot Church. The serenity of the corpse is most delightful! It preserves the sweet, benevolent smile which always distinguished him. They kindly press my

ABOVE *Miniature of George Austen, painted at the age of 70, a few years before his death. Jane wrote of 'the sweet, benevolent smile which always distinguished him.'*

mother to remove to Steventon as soon as it is all over, but I do not believe she will leave Bath at present . . .

We all unite in love, and I am affec:ly Yours *J.A.*

To Captain Francis Austen

GREEN PARK BGS. TUESDAY JANRY 29 [1805]

My dearest Frank

*M*Y MOTHER HAS FOUND AMONG our dear father's little personal property a small astronomical instrument, which she hopes you will accept for his sake. It is, I believe, a compass and sundial, and is in a black shagreen case. Would you have it sent to you now . . .? There is also a pair of scissors for you. We hope these are articles that may be useful to you, but we are sure they will be valuable. I have not time for more.

Yours very affecly. *J.A.*

LEFT *St Swithin's Walcot, where Jane's parents were married and Mr. Austen buried.*

GOODNESTONE FARM: FRIDAY AUGUST 30 [1805]

My dear Cassandra

BELOW Goodnestone, Kent, home of the Bridges family, from Vol. II of J. P. Neale's Views of the Seats of Noblemen and Gentlemen, 1826. Jane makes references to the famous local fair 'which makes its yearly distribution of gold paper and coloured persian through all the family connections'.

I HAVE DETERMINED ON staying here till Monday. Not that there is any occasion for it on Marianne's account, as she is now almost as well as usual, but Harriot is so kind in her wishes for my company that I could not resolve on leaving her tomorrow, especially as I had no reason to give for its necessity . . .

Edward Bridges dined at home yesterday; the day before he was at St. Albans; today he goes to Broome, and tomorrow to Mr. Hallett's, which latter engagement has had some weight in my resolution of not leaving Harriot till Monday.

Next week seems likely to be an unpleasant one to this family on the matter of game. The evil intentions of the Guards are certain, and the gentlemen of the neighbourhood seem unwilling to come forward in any decided or early support of their rights. Edward Bridges has been trying to arouse their spirits, but without success. Mr. Hammond, under the influence of daughters and an expected ball, declares he will do nothing . . .

I suppose everybody will be black for the D. of G. Must we buy lace, or will ribbon do? . . .

Yours affectionately, *J. A.*

Goodnestone Farm, near Canterbury was the home of Sir Brook Bridges' widow, Fanny, and her unmarried daughters. Marianne was an invalid; Harriot, the sixth daughter, later married George Moore of Wrotham. Edward Bridges probably proposed to Jane about now, and was rejected, which explains her relief at his absence at Mr. Hallett's — James Hallett of Higham, near Canterbury.

The puzzling reference to 'The evil intentions of the Guards' is explained by Dr. Chapman as follows: on 22 August Napoleon ordered his troops to begin their march from Boulogne to the Danube. On Friday 30th the Grenadier Guards marched from Deal to Chatham, passing the Coldstream and Scots Guards marching from Chatham to Deal. With partridge shooting due to begin the following Monday, poaching of the birds was anxiously feared; invasion by the French evidently not. Earlier in the summer Frank Austen, aboard the Leopard, *took part in the blockading of Boulogne, where an enormous flotilla of two thousand flat-bottomed boats awaited a favourable moment (which never came) to embark Napoleon's veteran troops on their way to England.*

William Hammond, of St. Alban's Court near Wigham, had five daughters. 'D. of G.' is a reference to the Duke of Gloucester.

ABOVE *Partridge shooting; print after Samuel Howitt for* Orme's Collection of British Field Sports, *1807.*

New Perspectives

LEFT *A view of Southampton and its walls; watercolour by Robert Ker Porter, 1797.*

After leaving Bath in July 1806 Mrs. Austen and her daughters spent the rest of the summer visiting their Leigh cousins at Adlestrop in Gloucestershire, moving on with them when the Reverend Thomas Leigh suddenly inherited, and took possession of, Stoneleigh Abbey in Warwickshire. The Abbey was enormous. Mrs. Austen wrote that the new owner 'almost despairs of ever finding his way about . . . I have proposed his setting up directing posts at the angles'. They next went on to stay at Hamstall Rectory in Staffordshire, where Jane caught whooping-cough from her little Cooper cousins.

By October they were installed, together with the Frank Austens, in lodgings in Southampton; and in March 1807 they all moved into a roomy, pleasant house in Castle Square, with a good garden. This was enclosed on one side by the old city wall, the top of which was quite wide enough to walk along, giving far-reaching views over Southampton Water to the Isle of Wight. The situation sounds delightful, and the whole arrangement had much to recommend it. The shared expenses were mutually beneficial; the presence of Martha Lloyd enabled Cassandra and Jane to go away on visits together, leaving their mother without anxiety; and Frank, with a new posting to convoy duty in the Far East, could confide his pregnant wife to the care and companionship of his mother and sisters.

In the first letters from Southampton Jane enjoyed plans for the new garden, but there were hints, too, of a slight depression: callers were a bit of a nuisance, and the Austen finances a worry.

ABOVE *'Southampton from Mr. Dance's'; watercolour by Edward Dayes.*

ABOVE *Portrait of Fanny Palmer at the time of her wedding to Charles Austen. The couple were married in Bermuda in 1807, when Fanny was 17. Her beautiful hair was her husband's 'especial delight'.*

RIGHT *Town plan of Southampton showing Castle Square, where the Austens lived, and the city walls bordering their garden, along which Jane liked to walk.*

Charles married seventeen-year-old Fanny Palmer in Bermuda in May 1807. Fanny was said to be plump and pretty with clouds of blond hair, although Jane later complained of Fanny's little daughter's looks being 'Palmerish'.

Between early 1807 and the summer of 1808 there is another gap in the letters, until Jane wrote in June from Godmersham, where she was spending three weeks – a short visit by the standards of the times. This letter gives a particularly strong impression of affectionate relations between the brothers and sisters. But, as with the other letters of this period, there is some sense of diminishment and the passage of time. The present visit did not seem quite so pleasant as an earlier one; and, worryingly, her pregnant sister-in-law Elizabeth did not look well.

In October it was Cassandra's turn to be at Godmersham, and it fell to her to give the shattering news of Elizabeth's sudden death after the birth of her eleventh child. Jane's next letters were full of anxiety and sorrow, added to a slightly macabre interest in the appearance of 'the corpse'. The hopes she expressed that 'dearest Fanny' would sustain her father were to be realised. Fanny was only fifteen at the time of her mother's death, but proved a capable manager of the enormous household and a kind and loving elder sister to the tribe of children. Edward never remarried, and Fanny remained mistress of Godmersham until 1820, when she married Sir Edward Knatchbull, handing the reigns over to her sister Marianne. Fanny held an increasingly special place in her Aunt Jane's heart. In a letter of 7 October, just before Elizabeth's death, Jane had written to Cassandra, 'I am greatly pleased with your account of Fanny; I found her in the summer just what you describe, almost another sister, and could not have supposed that a niece would ever have been so much to me . . . tell her that I always think of her with pleasure.'

Jane sent a loving account to Godmersham of Edward's two schoolboy sons, who spent a few days at Southampton over the period of their mother's funeral, entering into their sadness,

REFERENCES .

1   *Bar Gate & Guildhall*
2   *All Saints Church*
3   *East Gate*
4   *St Lawrence Church*
5   *Bridle Gate*
6   *Long Room*
7   *St Michael's Church*
8   *Holy Roods Conduit*
9   *Holy Rood Church*
10   *West Gate*
11   *Bugle Hall*
12   *St John's Hospital*
13   *The Theatre*
14   *Free School*
15   *Sugar House*
16   *Water Gate*
17   *Custom House*
18   *French Church*
19   *Gods House Hospital*
20   *Gods House Gate & Bridewell*
21   *New Gaol*
22   *Noah's Ark*
23   *St Mary's Church*
The intended Piers are coloured Yellow

sympathising with their anxiety to conform with convention over details of mourning clothes, and knowing when to divert their thoughts with games and outings.

In September 1808 Frank had returned from escorting troop ships to Portugal in the Peninsular campaign, and felt the need of a home of his own with his wife and baby. He took lodgings at Yarmouth on the Isle of Wight, leaving the Austen ladies and Martha Lloyd in Castle Square, now rather too large for their needs. Later in the autumn, however, Edward offered his mother the choice of two houses – either Chawton Cottage, on his second estate near Alton in Hampshire, or a house near Godmersham. The Austens chose the former: for one thing Henry had set up a branch of his banking enterprise in Alton; for another, it would mean a welcome return to a more familiar part of Hampshire. And Edward himself was taking more interest in his Hampshire property, moving his family to the Great House at Chawton for prolonged visits.

With this desirable change in view Jane's spirits evidently rose, and by the end of the year her letters spoke of plans to enjoy the remaining Southampton gaieties to the full and with a renewed sense of equilibrium. Writing on 9 December she exclaimed, 'It was the same room in which we danced fifteen years ago! I thought it all over – and in spite of the shame of being so much older, felt with thankfulness that I was quite as happy now as then.' A melancholy thought for the end of the year, provoked by Miss Murden, a difficult acquaintance, that – 'at her age, perhaps, one may be as friendless oneself, and in similar circumstances quite as captious', quickly turned to happy anticipations: 'Yes, yes, we *will* have a pianoforte, as good a one as can be got for thirty guineas, and I will practise country dances, that we may have some amusement for our nephews and nieces . . .'

Sir John Moore's death at Corunna was noticed in two letters of the time to Cassandra. Jane remarked, 'I wish Sir John had united something of the Christian with the hero in his death',

ABOVE *Portrait of Charles Austen, c.1809, painted in his naval uniform.*

evidently feeling that his dying thoughts should have focused on his God rather than on his fellow men. This is one of the scattered references to Jane's religious views which, taken together with her pleasure in reading sermons, and with the prayers she composed over the years, would seem to indicate a settled Christian faith.

The section ends with an attempt to retrieve the manuscript of *Susan* from Crosby, the publisher, who had not used it, but refused to relinquish it without payment. This first turning again towards literary activity may perhaps be thought of as the harbinger of the great creative period about to begin.

BELOW *Jane hoped to watch Frank skating as in this late eighteenth-century scene.*

SOUTHAMPTON: WEDNESDAY JANUARY 7 [1807]

My dear Cassandra

YOU WERE MISTAKEN IN supposing I should expect your letter on Sunday; I had no idea of hearing from you before Tuesday, and my pleasure yesterday was therefore unhurt by any previous disappointment. I thank you for writing so much; you must really have sent me the value of two letters in one. We are extremely glad to hear that Elizabeth is so much better, and hope you will be sensible of still further amendment in her when you return from Canterbury . . .

When you receive this, our guests will be all gone or going; and I shall be left to the comfortable disposal of my time, to ease of mind from the torments of rice puddings and apple dumplings, and probably to regret that I did not take more pains to please them all.

Mrs. J. Austen has asked me to return with her to Steventon; I need not give my answer; and she has invited my mother to spend there the time of Mrs. F. A.'s confinement, which she seems half inclined to do . . .

We did *not* take our walk on Friday, it was too dirty, nor have we yet done it; we may perhaps do something like it today, as after seeing Frank skate, which he hopes to do in the meadows . . . we are to treat ourselves with a passage over the ferry . . .

Our acquaintance increase too fast. He was recognised lately by Admiral Bertie, and a few days since arrived the Admiral and his daughter Catherine to wait upon us. There was nothing to like or dislike in either. To the Berties are to be added the Lances, with whose cards we have been endowed, and whose visit Frank and I returned yesterday . . .

Yours affectionately *J.A.*

The guests were James and Mary Austen and their little daughter Caroline. Jane now had two sisters-in-law called Mary, usually differentiating them as 'Mrs. J.A.' or 'Mrs. F.A.'.

BELOW *Skating scene showing the delightful conviviality of such occasions.*

63

SOUTHAMPTON FEB. 8 [1807]

My dearest Cassandra

*M*Y EXPECTATION OF HAVING nothing to say to you after the conclusion of my last seems nearer truth than I thought it would be, for I feel to have but little . . .

Our garden is putting in order by a man who bears a remarkably good character, has a very fine complexion, and asks something less than the first. The shrubs which border the gravel walk he says are only sweetbriar and roses, and the latter of an indifferent sort; we mean to get a few of a better kind therefore, and at my own particular desire he procures us some syringas. I could not do without a syringa, for the sake of Cowper's line. We talk also of a laburnum . . .

The morning was so wet that I was afraid we should not be able to see our little visitor, but Frank who alone could go to church called for her after service, and she is now talking away at my side and examining the treasures of my writing-desk drawers; very happy I believe. Not at all shy of course . . . What is become of all the shyness in the world? . . .

Eveng. Our little visitor has just left us, and left us highly pleased with her; she is a nice, natural, open hearted, affectionate girl, with all the ready civility which one sees in the best children of the present day; so unlike anything that I was myself at her age, that I am often all astonishment and shame . . .

Monday . . . I should not be surprised if we were to be visited by James again this week; he gave us reason to expect him soon, and if they go to Eversley he cannot come next week.

I am sorry and angry that his visits should not give one more pleasure; the company of so good and so dear a man ought to be gratifying in itself; but his chat seems all forced, his opinions on many points too much copied from his wife's, and his time here

ABOVE AND RIGHT *Gardeners at work from Pyne's* Microcosm. *'Our garden is putting in order by a man who bears a remarkably good character, has a very fine complexion, and asks something less than the first . . .'*

BELOW *Laburnum from Curtis's* Botanical Magazine.

BELOW LEFT *Syringa Vulgaris or common lilac. Curtis wrote, 'Few shrubs are better known in this country than the lilac, few more universally cultivated; there is scarcely a cottage it does not enliven, or a shrubbery it does not beautify.'*

is spent I think in walking about the house and banging the doors, or ringing the bell for a glass of water.

There, I flatter myself I have constructed you a smartish letter, considering my want of materials, but like my dear Dr. Johnson I believe I have dealt more in notions than facts . . .

Yrs affectely *J.A.*

The garden was at the Castle Square house, Southampton. 'Cowper's line' is 'Laburnum, rich/In streaming gold; syringa, iv'ry pure' (The Task). The 'little visitor' was Catherine, child of Captain Foote of Highfield House, Southampton.

GODMERSHAM: WEDNESDAY JUNE 15 [1808]

My dear Cassandra

WHERE SHALL I BEGIN? Which of all my important nothings shall I tell you first? At half after seven yesterday morning Henry saw us into our own carriage, and we drove away from the Bath hotel; which, by the by, had been found most uncomfortable quarters – very dirty, very noisy, and very ill-provided . . . At Dartford, which we reached within the two hours and three-quarters, we went to the Bull, the same inn at which we breakfasted in that said journey, and on the present occasion had about the same bad butter.

At half-past ten we were again off, and, travelling on without any adventure reached Sittingbourne by three . . . A few minutes, of course, did for Sittingbourne; and so off we drove, drove, drove, and by six o'clock were at Godmersham.

Our two brothers were walking before the house as we approached, as natural as life. Fanny and Lizzy met us in the Hall with a great deal of pleasant joy; we went for a few minutes into

BELOW *Miniature of James Austen, Jane's eldest brother, who succeeded his father to the living of Steventon.*

BELOW *A farmyard scene from Pyne's* Microcosm. *Note the multi-purpose breeding house reminiscent of Noah's ark.*

BELOW *A farmyard scene from Pyne's* Microcosm. *Note the multi-purpose breeding house reminiscent of Noah's ark.*

the breakfast parlour, and then proceeded to our rooms. Mary has the hall chamber. I am in the yellow room – very literally – for I am writing in it at this moment. It seems odd to me to have such a great place all to myself, and to be at Godmersham without you is also odd.

Elizabeth, who was dressing when we arrived, came to me for a minute attended by Marianne, Charles and Louisa, and, you will not doubt, gave me a very affectionate welcome. That I had received such from Edward also I need not mention; but I do, you see, because it is a pleasure. I never saw him look in better health, and Fanny says he is perfectly well. I cannot praise Elizabeth's looks, but they are probably affected by a cold . . .

Thursday . . . Yesterday passed quite à la Godmersham: the gentlemen rode about Edward's farm, and returned in time to saunter along Bentigh with us; and after dinner we visited the Temple Plantations, which, to be sure, is a Chevalier Bayard of a plantation. James and Mary are much struck with the beauty of the place. Today the spirit of the thing is kept up by the two brothers being gone to Canterbury in the chair . . .

I feel rather languid and solitary – perhaps because I have a cold; but three years ago we were more animated with you and Harriot and Miss Sharpe. We shall improve, I dare say, as we go on.

Friday . . . I have a great deal of love to give from everybody.

Yours most affectionately, *Jane*

Jane was paying a visit to Godmersham in company with the James Austens and their two younger children. Fanny and Lizzy were the two eldest daughters of the house; Marianne, Charles and Louisa three more of Edward's large family. Elizabeth was pregnant with her eleventh child. Harriot (Bridges) was Elizabeth's sister; Anne Sharpe had been governess to the Godmersham children.

RIGHT *Godmersham from* Views of the Noblemen's and Gentlemen's Seats of Kent *by J. G. Wood, 1800.*

GODMERSHAM, THURSDAY JUNE 30 [1808]

My dear Cassandra

I GIVE YOU ALL JOY of Frank's return, which happens in the true sailor way, just after our being told not to expect him for some weeks. The wind has been very much against him, but I suppose he must be in our neighbourhood by this time; Fanny is in hourly expectation of him here . . .

We want you to send us Anna's height, that we may know whether she is as tall as Fanny; and pray can you tell me of any little thing that would be probably acceptable to Mrs. F. A.? I wish to bring her something; has she a silver knife — or would you recommend a brooch? I shall not spend more than half a guinea about it . . .

So much was written before breakfast; it is now half-past twelve, and having heard Lizzy read, I am moved down into the library for the sake of a fire, which agreeably surprised us when we assembled at ten, and here in warm and happy solitude proceed to acknowledge this day's letter . . .

In another week I shall be at home and then, my having been at Godmersham will seem like a dream.

The orange wine will want our care soon. But in the meantime, for elegance and ease and luxury; the Hattons and Milles dine here today — and I shall eat ice and drink French wine, and be above vulgar economy. Luckily the pleasures of friendship, of unreserved conversation, of similarity of taste and opinions, will make good amends for orange wine . . .

Yrs affec:ly with love from all, *J. A.*

Jane helped her sister-in-law with the children's lessons, hearing Lizzy read, as they were between governesses.

ABOVE *Late eighteenth-century engraving of the West Gate of Canterbury. In her widowhood Mrs. Knight retired from Godmersham, which she had made over to Edward, to White Friars in Canterbury, where Jane visited her. 'Mrs. K. was alone in her drawing room, as gentle and kind and friendly as usual.'*

BELOW *Pen and ink drawing by Rowlandson of a funeral procession. Elizabeth Knight's funeral from Godmersham would have looked somewhat similar. Jane wrote, 'Tomorrow will be a dreadful day for you all . . . Glad shall I be to hear it is over.'*

CASTLE SQUARE, OCTR. 13 [1808]

My dearest Cassandra

I HAVE RECEIVED YOUR LETTER, and with most melancholy anxiety was it expected, for the sad news reached us last night, but without any particulars; it came in a short letter to Martha from her sister, begun at Steventon, and finished in Winchester.

We have felt, we do feel, for you all – as you will not need to be told – for you, for Fanny, for Henry, for Lady Bridges, and for dearest Edward, whose loss and whose sufferings seem to make those of every other person nothing. God be praised! that you can say what you do of him – that he has a religious mind to bear him up, and a disposition that will gradually lead him to comfort.

My dear, dear Fanny! I am so thankful that she has you with her! You will be everything to her, you will give her all the consolation that human aid can give. May the Almighty sustain you all – and keep you my dearest Cassandra well – but for the present I dare say you are equal to everything.

You will know that the poor boys are at Steventon. Perhaps it is best for them, as they will have more means of exercise and amusement there than they could have with us, but I own myself disappointed by the arrangement; I should have loved to have them with me at such a time. I shall write to Edward by this post . . . I long to hear more of you all . . .

Farewell for the present, my dearest sister. Tell Edward that we feel for him and pray for him.

Yrs affectely *J. A*usten

Edward's wife, Elizabeth, died suddenly on 10 October 1808. The 'poor boys' were young Edward and George. They were at Winchester College, but had a few days' compassionate leave.

RIGHT *Mourning clothes for woman and child from Ackermann's Repository. 'I shall send you such of your mourning as I think most likely to be useful, reserving for myself your stockings and half the velvet, in which selfish arrangement I know I am doing what you wish. I am to be in bombasine and crêpe, according to what we are told is universal here,' Jane wrote to Cassandra on their sister-in-law's death.*

CASTLE SQUARE, SATURDAY NIGHT OCTR. 15 [1808]

My dear Cassandra

*Y*OUR ACCOUNTS MAKE US as comfortable as we can expect to be at such a time . . .

Your account of Lizzy is very interesting. Poor child! One must hope the impression *will* be strong, and yet one's heart aches for a dejected mind of eight years old.

I suppose you see the corpse? How does it appear? We are anxious to be assured that Edward will not attend the funeral, but when it comes to the point, I think he must feel it impossible . . . I shall send you such of your mourning as I think most likely to be useful, reserving for myself your stockings and half the velvet, in which selfish arrangement I know I am doing what you wish. I am to be in bombasine and crêpe . . .

Sunday . . . That you are for ever in our thoughts you will not doubt. I see your mournful party in my mind's eye under every varying circumstance of the day; and in the evening especially, figure to myself its sad gloom – the efforts to talk – the frequent summons to melancholy orders and cares – and poor Edward, restless in misery, going from one room to another – and perhaps not seldom upstairs, to see all that remains of his Elizabeth . . .

Adieu. You cannot write too often, as I said before. We are heartily rejoiced that the poor baby gives you no particular anxiety. Kiss dear Lizzy for us. Tell Fanny that I shall write in a day or two to Miss Sharpe.

Yours most truly *J. Austen*

CASTLE SQUARE: MONDAY OCTOBER 24 [1808]

My dear Cassandra

*E*DWARD AND GEORGE CAME to us soon after seven on Saturday, very well, but very cold, having by choice travelled on the outside, and with no great coat but what Mr. Wise, the coachman, good-naturedly spared them of his . . .

They behave extremely well in every respect, showing quite as much feeling as one wishes to see, and on every occasion speaking of their father with the liveliest affection. His letter was read over by each of them yesterday, and with many tears; George sobbed aloud, Edward's tears do not flow so easily; but as far as I can judge they are both very properly impressed by what has happened . . .

We do not want amusement: bilbocatch, at which George is indefatigable, spillikins, paper ships, riddles, conundrums, and cards, with watching the flow and ebb of the river, and now and then a stroll out, keep us well employed; and we mean to avail ourselves of our kind papa's consideration, by not returning to Winchester till quite the evening of Wednesday . . .

Edward has an old black coat, which will save *his* having a second new one; but I find that black pantaloons are considered by them as necessary, and of course one would not have them made uncomfortable by the want of what is usual on such occasions . . .

While I write now, George is most industriously making and naming paper ships, at which he afterwards shoots with horse-chestnuts, brought from Steventon on purpose; and Edward equally intent over the 'Lake of Killarney,' twisting himself about in one of our great chairs.

Tuesday . . . Of Chawton I think I can have nothing more to say, but that everything you say about it in the letter now before me

BELOW *Ackermann writes of this Winchester scholar, 'The annexed print does not, in every respect, exhibit the statutable costume; nor would any scholar presume to come before the warden in white pantaloons; nor with his gown otherwise than closed.'*

will, I am sure, as soon as I am able to read it to her, make my mother consider the plan with more and more pleasure . . .

We have just had two hampers of apples from Kintbury, and the floor of our little garret is almost covered. Love to all.

Yours very affectionately, *J. A.*

CASTLE SQUARE, FRIDAY DECR. 9 [1808]

*M*ANY THANKS, MY DEAR Cassandra, to you and Mr. Deedes for your joint and agreeable composition, which took me by surprise this morning . . .

A larger circle of acquaintance, and an increase of amusement, is quite in character with our approaching removal. Yes – I mean to go to as many balls as possible, that I may have a good bargain. Everybody is very much concerned at our going away, and everybody is acquainted with Chawton, and speaks of it as a remarkably pretty village, and everybody knows the house we describe – but nobody fixes on the right.

I am very much obliged to Mrs. Knight for such a proof of the interest she takes in me, and she may depend upon it that I *will* marry Mr. Papillon, whatever may be his reluctance or my own. I owe her much more than such a trifling sacrifice.

Our ball was rather more amusing than I expected, Martha liked it very much, and I did not gape till the last quarter of an hour. It was past nine before we were sent for, and not twelve when we returned. The room was tolerably full, and there were perhaps thirty couple of dancers. The melancholy part was to see so many dozen young women standing by without partners, and each of them with two ugly naked shoulders!

It was the same room in which we danced fifteen years ago! I thought it all over – and in spite of the shame of being so much older, felt with thankfulness that I was quite as happy now as

then. We paid an additional shilling for our tea, which we took as we chose in an adjoining and very comfortable room.

There were only four dances, and it went to my heart that the Miss Lances (one of them, too, named Emma!) should have partners only for two. You will not expect to hear that *I* was asked to dance – but I was – by the gentleman whom we met *that Sunday* with Captain d'Auvergne. We have always kept up a bowing acquaintance since, and being pleased with his black eyes, I spoke to him at the ball, which brought on me this civility; but I do not know his name, and he seems so little at home in the English language, that I believe his black eyes may be the best of him . . .

I am glad you are to have Henry with you again; with him and the boys you cannot but have a cheerful, and at times even a merry, Christmas . . .

Distribute the affectionate love of a heart not so tired as the right hand belonging to it.

Yours ever sincerely *J.A.*

Mr. Papillon was the bachelor rector of Chawton, considered by Mrs. Knight to be a suitable husband for Jane.

"MRS. JENNINGS was a widow, with an ample jointure. She had only two daughters, both of whom she had lived to see respectably married, and she had now therefore nothing to do but to marry all the rest of the world. In the promotion of this object she was zealously active, as far as her ability reached; and missed no opportunity of projecting weddings among all the young people of her acquaintance. She was remarkably quick in the discovery of attachments, and had enjoyed the advantage of raising the blushes and the vanity of many a young lady by

Mrs. Jennings the matchmaker embarrasses Marianne Dashwood.

insinuations of her power over such a young man; and this kind of discernment enabled her soon after her arrival at Barton decisively to pronounce that Colonel Brandon was very much in love with Marianne Dashwood . . . It must be so. She was perfectly convinced of it. It would be an excellent match, for *he* was rich and *she* was handsome. **"**

SENSE AND SENSIBILITY

CASTLE SQUARE, TUESDAY DEC. 27 [1808]

My dear Cassandra

I CAN NOW WRITE AT leisure and make the most of my subjects, which is lucky, as they are not numerous this week . . .

Lady Sondes' match surprises, but does not offend me; had her first marriage been of affection, or had there been a grown-up single daughter, I should not have forgiven her; but I consider everybody as having a right to marry *once* in their lives for love if they can – and provided she will now leave off having bad headaches and being pathetic, I can allow her, I can *wish* her, to be happy . . .

Our evening party on Thursday produced nothing more remarkable than Miss Murden's coming too, though she had declined it absolutely in the morning, and sitting very ungracious and very silent with us from seven o'clock till half after eleven, for so late was it, owing to the chairmen, before we got rid of them.

The last hour, spent in yawning and shivering in a wide circle round the fire, was dull enough – but the tray had admirable success. The widgeon and the preserved ginger were as delicious as one could wish. But as to our black butter, do not decoy anybody to Southampton by such a lure, for it is all gone . . .

ABOVE, LEFT AND FAR LEFT The Code of Terpsichore *by C. Blasis demonstrating something of the grace of contemporary dance movements. All the drawings illustrate 'The Manner of Taking Hands in the Quadrille'.*

Wednesday . . . Miss Murden was quite a different creature this last evening from what she had been before, owing to her having with Martha's help found a situation in the morning, which bids very fair for comfort. When she leaves Steventon, she comes to board and lodge with Mrs. Hookey, the chemist – for there is no Mr. Hookey. I cannot say that I am in any hurry for the conclusion of her present visit, but I was truly glad to see her comfortable in mind and spirits; at her age, perhaps, one may be as friendless oneself, and in similar circumstances quite as captious . . .

Yes, yes, we *will* have a pianoforte, as good a one as can be got for thirty guineas, and I will practise country dances, that we may have some amusement for our nephews and nieces, when we have the pleasure of their company.

Fare you well.

Yrs. affecly. *J. Austen*

Lady Sondes was to marry General Sir Henry Montresor. Black butter or apple butter was 'a simple, uncostly and delightful conserve'. Miss Murden was a spinster acquaintance grumbled over but befriended by Cassandra and Jane.

BELOW *A Regency engraving showing a lady's pianoforte, a precious possession.*

66 'But then, to be an old maid at last, like Miss Bates!'

'That is as formidable an image as you could present, Harriet; and if I thought I should ever be like Miss Bates! so silly – so satisfied – so smiling – so prosing – so undistinguishing and unfastidious – and so apt to tell every thing relative to every body about me, I would marry tomorrow. But between *us*, I am convinced there never can be any likeness, except in being unmarried.'

'But still, you will be an old maid! And that's so dreadful!'

'Never mind, Harriet, I shall not be a poor old maid; and

Emma's views on the blessings of a single state for the well-endowed.

it is poverty only which makes celibacy contemptible to a generous public! A single woman, with a very narrow income, must be a ridiculous, disagreeable old maid! The proper sport of boys and girls; but a single woman, of good fortune, is always respectable, and may be as sensible and pleasant as anybody else.' **"**

EMMA

BELOW *A postman from Pyne's* The Costume of Great Britain.

CASTLE SQUARE TUESDAY JANY. 24 [1809]

My dear Cassandra

I WILL GIVE YOU THE indulgence of a letter on Thursday this week, instead of Friday, but I do not require you to write again before Sunday, provided I may believe you and your finger going on quite well. Take care of your precious self; do not work too hard. Remember that Aunt Cassandras are quite as scarce as Miss Beverleys.

I had the happiness yesterday of a letter from Charles, but I shall say as little about it as possible, because I know *that* excruciating Henry will have had a letter likewise, to make all my intelligence valueless. It was written at Bermuda on the 7th and 10th of December. All well, and Fanny still only in expectation of being otherwise. He had taken a small prize in his late cruise – a French schooner laden with sugar, but bad weather parted them, and she had not yet been heard of . . .

You rejoice me by what you say of Fanny – I hope she will not turn good-for-nothing this ever so long. We thought of and talked of her yesterday with sincere affection, and wished her a long enjoyment of all the happiness to which she seems born. While she gives happiness to those about her she is pretty sure of her own share.

I am gratified by her having pleasure in what I write, but I wish the knowledge of my being exposed to her discerning criticism may not hurt my style, by inducing too great a solicitude. I begin already to weigh my words and sentences more than I did, and am looking about for a sentiment, an illustration, or a metaphor in every corner of the room. Could my ideas flow as fast as the rain in the store closet it would be charming.

We have been in two or three dreadful states within the last week, from the melting of the snow etc., and the contest between us and the closet has now ended in our defeat. I have been obliged to move almost everything out of it, and leave it to splash itself as it likes . . .

You depend upon finding all your plants dead, I hope. They look very ill,
I understand . . .

RIGHT *The death of General Sir John Moore at Corunna in 1809.*

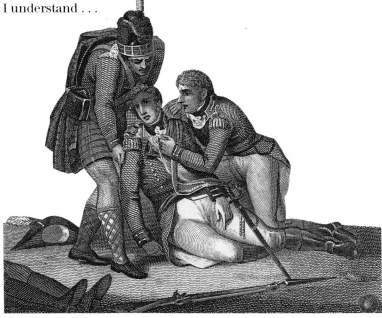

Adieu, sweet you. This is grievous news from Spain. It is well that Dr. Moore was spared the knowledge of such a son's death.

Yrs. affecly. *J. A*usten

Miss Beverley was the heroine of Fanny Burney's Cecilia. *'Such a son's death' refers to Sir John Moore who died at Corunna.*

TO CROSBIE [CROSBY] & CO.

Gentlemen,

*I*N THE SPRING OF the year 1803 a MS. novel in two vol. entitled Susan, was sold to you by a gentleman of the name of Seymour, and the purchase money £10 recd. at the same time. Six years have since passed, and this work, of which I am myself the authoress, has never to the best of my knowledge appeared in print, tho' an early publication was stipulated for at the time of sale. I can only account for such an extraordinary circumstance by supposing the MS. by some carelessness to have been lost, and if that was the case am willing to supply you with another copy if you are disposed to avail yourselves of it, and will engage for no farther delay when it comes into your hands . . . Should no notice be taken of this address, I shall feel myself at liberty to secure the publication of my work by applying elsewhere.

I am Gentlemen etc., etc. *M. A. D.*

Direct to Mrs. Ashton Dennis, Post Office, Southampton 5 April 1809.

Crosby returned a disobliging reply to this plea, written by Jane under the pseudonym of Mrs. Ashton Dennis.

CHAWTON 1809–1813

A New and Settled Home

This group of letters begins with an ebullient poem combining congratulations to Frank on the birth of a son with happy exultation over the new home: 'when complete/It will all other houses beat'. Chawton Cottage is still very pleasant today, square and solid, with well-proportioned sunny rooms giving an impression of space and calm. In Jane's day the garden was larger, and the main Winchester road passed under the front windows. Mrs. Thomas Knight wrote to Fanny soon after the Austens were settled into the cottage, 'I heard of the Chawton party looking very comfortable at breakfast, from a gentleman who was travelling by their door in a post-chaise about ten days since.'

Life otherwise was somewhat circumscribed: Mrs. Austen could not afford to keep a carriage (although later she acquired a donkey and cart), so social activities had to be confined to those within walking distance. Cassandra and Jane continued to pay long visits to their relations, but only when their brothers could transport them. On the other hand Chawton was less than a day's ride across the fields from Steventon, so that James, with his daughter Anna, could come to see his mother and sisters; Edward and his family frequently stayed at the Great House; and nearer to Alton, at Rose Cottage, were Frank's wife and baby.

For Jane this was the beginning of the great creative years, which were to bring her much satisfaction and a modest fame. At first she was anxious to remain anonymous, but when this

ABOVE *Mrs. Thomas Knight as a young woman by George Romney.*

BELOW *Sweet William. Jane wrote from Chawton in May 1811, 'The whole of the shrubbery garden will soon be very gay with pinks and sweet-williams.'*

proved impossible her letters give an impression of wry enjoyment at her new status as a literary figure.

Some of her nieces were now old enough to retain impressions of their aunt which they would later record. Caroline Austen left a description of her Aunt Jane: 'Her charm to children was her great sweetness of manner – she seemed to love you and you loved her naturally in return . . . Then, as I got older, and when cousins came to share the entertainment, she would tell us the most delightful stories chiefly of fairyland, and her fairies all had characters of their own. The tale was invented, I am sure, at the moment, and was sometimes continued for two or three days, if occasion served.' Caroline remembered her aunts as 'not accounted very good dressers . . . but particularly neat.' She commented on the cheerfulness and harmony of the household: 'it was not their habit to argue with each other'.

The day would begin with Jane playing her piano, so as not to disturb the others later on. Her particular household task was then to get the breakfast. She and Cassandra had by now taken on the housekeeping, leaving Mrs. Austen to the sewing and gardening. The latter was not just ladylike weeding, but included digging potatoes, dressed in a labourer's smock.

Apart from afternoon walks to pay calls on neighbours, or to shop in Alton, much of Jane's time was now spent in writing. If callers appeared, little sheets of manuscript were quickly slipped under her blotter; and the sitting room door had a noisy squeak, which remained unrepaired (as it still has), so that she could have a moment's warning of their approach.

During the years covered by these letters *Sense and Sensibility* and *Pride and Prejudice* were published, and *Mansfield Park* written. Henry was helpful over negotiations with publishers and printers, and Jane stayed with him and Eliza in Sloane Street to correct her proofs. She enjoyed these visits and the parties and theatre-goings they entailed, and was amused to meet such exotic friends of Eliza's as the emigré comte d'Entraigues and his wife,

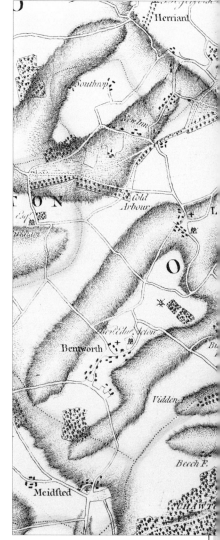

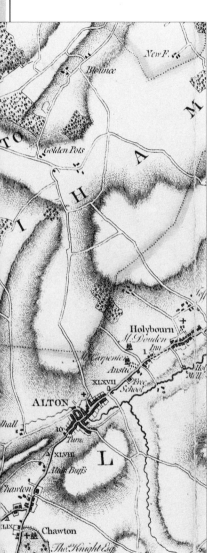

an opera singer. Both were murdered the next year by their manservant, and rumour had it that the comte had been an experienced double agent.

Jane also liked going to exhibitions, and wrote to Cassandra of her excitement at finding a portrait of Mrs. Bingley (Jane Bennet in *Pride and Prejudice*) in one of the galleries. Her characters were always very real to her, and her nephew James remembered that she would sometimes give extra pieces of information about them: the 'considerable sum' Mrs. Norris gave William Price as a tip in *Mansfield Park*, for instance, was one pound; Kitty Bennet married a clergyman near Pemberley; and Mr. Woodhouse lived for two years after Emma's marriage.

In April 1813 Eliza Austen died in Sloane Street after a long illness. Jane was with her, and afterwards spent a good deal of time with Henry, trying to help him over his bereavement. In 1812 old Mrs. Knight died, and Edward and his family formally took on the name of Knight, much to the irritation of Fanny, who would have preferred to remain Austen.

Early in 1813 *Pride and Prejudice*, Jane's 'own darling child', appeared, to excellent reviews, becoming the most successful novel of the season, and counting the Prince Regent, Warren Hastings and Sheridan among its many admirers. By now Jane was working on *Mansfield Park*. She had Northamptonshire in mind as the setting for the new novel, and possibly Cottesbrooke Hall, which belonged to Henry's friend Sir James Langham, as the model for the house itself. On 29 January 1813 she wrote to Cassandra, 'If you cd. discover whether Northamptonshire is a country of hedgerows, I shd. be glad again.' She may have been contemplating a scene in which one character would overhear a conversation taking place on the other side of a hedge, such as was later to appear in *Persuasion*.

The Knight family were at the Great House that summer, and Fanny and Jane spent much time together, to their mutual pleasure. Fanny's younger sister, Marianne, was jealous of their

LEFT *Detail of Milne's map of Hampshire, 1791, showing some of Jane Austen's walks in the neighbourhood.*

intimacy and resented her exclusion from the readings of *Pride and Prejudice* which went on behind the closed bedroom door, punctuated with gusts of laughter. All the nieces were agreed on the excellence of Jane's reading aloud. Marianne also remembered how her aunt, during a visit to Godmersham, would sit 'quietly working beside the fire in the library, saying nothing for a good while, and then would suddenly burst out laughing, jump up and run across the room to a table where pens and paper were lying, write something down, and then come back to the fire and go on quietly working as before'. 'Working' in this context would have meant needlework.

In July 1813 Anna became engaged to Ben Lefroy, and her aunt felt a little anxious about their differing temperaments. The marriage in the event turned out well (and fruitfully: one son and six daughters).

Jane spent two months at Godmersham in the autumn, which proved to be her last visit there. Writing to Cassandra she described the constant bustle of a large house party, expressing her especial pleasure in the occasional lulls when 'my Br., Fanny and I have the Library to ourselves in delightful quiet'. This letter is the last in the group, belonging to a period of renewed hope and peerless work, of happy involvement with the ramifications of her family and of personal satisfaction and increasing artistic maturity.

BELOW AND RIGHT *Ladies enjoying gentle occupations as evoked by the early nineteenth-century artist, John Harden.*

To Francis Austen

CHAWTON, JULY 26 [1809]

*M*Y DEAREST FRANK, I wish you joy
Of Mary's safety with a boy,
Whose birth has given little pain
Compared with that of Mary Jane.
May he a growing blessing prove,
And well deserve his parents' love!
Endow'd with Art's and Nature's good,
Thy name possessing with thy blood,
In him, in all his ways, may we
Another Francis William see!
Thy infant days may he inherit,
Thy warmth, nay insolence of spirit;
We would not with one fault dispense
To weaken the resemblance . . .

As for ourselves we're very well;
As unaffected prose will tell.
Cassandra's pen will paint our state,
The many comforts that await
Our Chawton home, how much we find
Already in it, to our mind;
And how convinced, that when complete
It will all other houses beat
That ever have been made or mended,
With rooms concise, or rooms distended.
You'll find us very snug next year,
Perhaps with Charles and Fanny near,
For now it often does delight us
To fancy them just over-right us.

BELOW AND RIGHT *Examples of Jane Austen's handwriting, including part of this ode in celebration of the Austens' arrival at Chawton Cottage.*

BELOW *The British Museum, the new building depicted in* Ackermann's Repository *for April 1810.*

BELOW *A miniature of Jane's dashing cousin Eliza, painted during her marriage to the comte de Feuillide.*

SLOANE ST. THURSDAY APRIL 18 [1811]

My dear Cassandra

I HAVE SO MANY LITTLE matters to tell you of, that I cannot wait any longer before I begin to put them down . . .

Mary and I, after disposing of her father and mother, went to the Liverpool Museum and the British Gallery, and I had some amusement at each, tho' my preference for men and women always inclines me to attend more to the company than the sight . . .

I did not see Theo. till late on Tuesday; he was gone to Ilford, but he came back in time to shew his usual, nothing-meaning, harmless, heartless civility. Henry, who had been confined the whole day to the bank, took me in his way home; and after putting life and wit into the party for a quarter of an hour, put himself and his sister into a hackney coach . . .

I am sorry to tell you that I am getting very extravagant and spending all my money; and what is worse for *you*, I have been spending yours too; for in a linendraper's shop to which I went for check'd muslin, and for which I was obliged to give seven shillings a yard, I was tempted by a pretty coloured muslin, and bought ten yds. of it, on the chance of your liking it; but at the same time, if it shd. not suit you, you must not think yourself at all obliged to take it; it is only 3/6 pr. yd., and I shd. not in the least mind keeping the whole. In texture, it is just what we prefer, but its resemblance to green crewels I must own is not great, for the pattern is a small red spot . . .

We drank tea again yesterday with the Tilsons, and met the Smiths. I find all these little parties very pleasant . . .

Eliza is walking out by herself. She has plenty of business on her hands just now – for the day of the party is settled, and drawing near; above 80 people are invited for next Tuesday eveng. and there is to be some very good music, five professionals, three of them glee singers, besides amateurs. Fanny will listen to this. One of the hirelings is a capital on the harp, from which I expect great pleasure . . .

Saturday . . . If the weather permits, Eliza and I walk into London this morng. *She* is in want of chimney lights for Tuesday; and I of an ounce of darning cotton. She has resolved not to venture to the play tonight. The d'Entraigues and comte Julien cannot come to the party – which was at first a grief, but she has since supplied herself so well with performers that it is of no consequence; their not coming has produced our going to them tomorrow eveng. – which I like the idea of. It will be amusing to see the ways of a French circle . . .

Love to all.

Yours affec: *Jane*

'Theo.' was the Reverend Theophilus Cooke. 'Crewels' were worsted designs embroidered on linen or cloth. James Tilson was a partner in Henry's banking firm, Austen, Maunde and Tilson. The Henry Austens were living in Sloane Street, which was then a long, tree-lined road leading from the village of Chelsea to the main thoroughfare into London itself. The d'Entraigues were French friends of Eliza's.

BELOW *Swatches of fabric stuck into Ackermann's* Repository *for May 1812; including a new and ingenious invention for ladies' hats composed of willow shavings.*

RIGHT *Drapers Harding Howell & Co., from Ackermann's* Repository *for March 1809. Ackermann wrote, 'Immediately at the entrance is the first department, which is exclusively appropriated to the sale of furs and fans. The second contains articles of haberdashery of every description, silks, muslin, lace, gloves, etc.'*

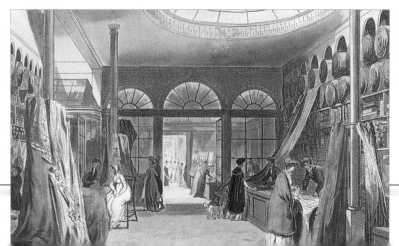

SLOANE ST. THURSDAY APRIL 25 [1811]

My dearest Cassandra

BELOW *A harpist 'in concert room full dress'. A harpist was much in demand at parties such as Eliza Austen's in Sloane Street. 'One of the hirelings, is a capital on the harp, from which I expect great pleasure,' Jane told Cassandra.*

I CAN RETURN THE COMPLIMENT by thanking you for the unexpected pleasure of *your* letter yesterday, and as I like unexpected pleasure, it made me very happy . . .

No, indeed, I am never too busy to think of S. and S. I can no more forget it than a mother can forget her sucking child; and I am much obliged to you for your enquiries. I have had two sheets to correct, but the last only brings us to W.'s first appearance . . . Henry does not neglect it; he *has* hurried the printer and says he will see him again today . . . I am very much gratified by Mrs. K.'s interest in it; and whatever may be the event of it as to my credit with her, sincerely wish her curiosity could be satisfied sooner than is now probable. I think she will like my Elinor, but cannot build on anything else.

Our party went off extremely well. There were many solicitudes, alarms and vexations beforehand . . . but at last everything was quite right. The rooms were dressed up with flowers etc., and looked very pretty . . . Mr. Egerton and Mr. Walter came at ½ past 5 and the festivities began with a pr. of very fine soles.

At ½ past 7 arrived the musicians in two hackney coaches, and by 8 the lordly company began to appear. Among the earliest were George and Mary Cooke, and I spent the greatest part of the eveng. very pleasantly with them. The drawg. room being soon hotter than we liked, we placed ourselves in the connecting passage, which was comparatively cool, and gave us all the advantage of the music at a pleasant distance, as well as that of the first view of every new comer . . .

My mother and Martha both write with great satisfaction of Anna's behaviour. She is quite an Anna with variations but she cannot have reached her last, for that is always the most flourishing and shewy – she is at about her 3d or 4th which are generally simple and pretty.

We *did* go to the play after all on Saturday. We went to the Lyceum, and saw the Hypocrite, an old play taken from Molière's Tartuffe, and were well entertained . . .

BELOW *The Lyceum, a contemporary engraving.*

Eliza caught her cold on Sunday in our way to the d'Entraigues; the horses actually jibbed on this side of Hyde Park Gate – a load of fresh gravel made it a formidable hill to them and they refused the collar; I believe there was a sore shoulder to irritate. Eliza was frightened and we got out – and were detained in the eveng. air several minutes . . .

Eliza enjoyed her eveng. very much, and means to cultivate the acquaintance – and I see nothing to dislike in them, but their taking quantities of snuff. Monsieur the old Count, is a very fine looking man, with quiet manners, good enough for an Englishman, and, I believe, is a man of great information and taste. He has some fine paintings, which delighted Henry as much as the son's music gratified Eliza . . .

Yrs. affecly. *J.A.*

The 'new nephew' was Frank's baby son, Henry. 'S. and S.' was Sense and Sensibility; 'W.', Willoughby in that novel. 'Mrs. K.' was Mrs. Knight.

LEFT *Thomas Rowlandson's drawing of the Serpentine in Hyde Park where Jane enjoyed promenading during her London visits.*

CHAWTON FRIDAY MAY 31 [1811]

My dear Cassandra

*I*HAVE A MAGNIFICENT PROJECT. The Cookes have put off their visit to us . . .

This circumstance has made me think the present time would be favourable for Miss Sharpe coming to us . . . and if you and Martha do not dislike the plan, and she can avail herself of it, the opportunity of her being conveyed hither will be excellent . . .

From Monday to Wednesday Anna is to be engaged at Faringdon, in order that she may come in for the gaieties of Tuesday (ye 4th), on Selborne Common, where there are to be volunteers and felicities of all kinds . . .

Have you remembered to collect pieces for the patchwork? We are now at a stand-still . . .

You cannot imagine – it is not in human nature to imagine what a nice walk we have round the orchard. The row of beech look very well indeed, and so does the young quickset hedge in

RIGHT *The village of Selborne, a late eighteenth-century watercolour by S. H. Grimm.*

the garden. I hear today that an apricot has been detected on one of the trees . . .

God bless you, and I hope June will find you well and bring us together.

Yrs. Ever *J*ane

The 'gaieties of Tuesday (ye 4th)' were in celebration of George III's birthday, still kept as a holiday at Eton College. The patchwork quilt made by the Austen ladies can be seen at Chawton.

BELOW *The patchwork made by Jane and her mother. 'Have you remembered to collect pieces for the patchwork?' Jane asked.*

Mrs. Norris defends her apricot tree.

66 'It was only the spring twelvemonth before Mr. Norris's death, that we put in the apricot against the stable wall, which is now grown such a noble tree, and getting to such perfection, sir,' addressing herself then to Dr. Grant.

'The tree thrives well beyond a doubt, madam,' replied Dr. Grant. 'The soil is good; and I never pass it without regretting, that the fruit should be so little worth the trouble of gathering.'

'Sir, it is a moor park, we bought it as a moor park, and it cost us — that is, it was a present from Sir Thomas, but I saw the bill, and I know it cost seven shillings, and was charged as a moor park.'

'You were imposed on, ma'am,' replied Dr. Grant; 'these potatoes have as much the flavour of a moor park apricot, as the fruit from that tree. It is an insipid fruit at the best; but a good apricot is eatable, which none from my garden are . . .'

Dr. Grant and Mrs. Norris were seldom good friends; their acquaintance had begun in dilapidations, and their habits were totally dissimilar. 99

MANSFIELD PARK

CHAWTON THURSDAY JUNE 6 [1811]

*B*Y THIS TIME MY dearest Cassandra, you know Martha's plans. I was rather disappointed I confess to find that she could not leave town till after ye 24th, as I had hoped to see you here the week before . . .

I had a few lines from Henry on Tuesday to prepare us for himself and his friend, and by the time that I had made the sumptuous provision of a neck of mutton on the occasion, they drove into the court – but lest you should not immediately recollect in how many hours a neck of mutton may be certainly procured, I add that they came a little after twelve – both tall and well, and in their different degrees agreeable.

It was a visit of only twenty-four hours – but very pleasant while it lasted. Mr. Tilson took a sketch of the Great House before dinner; and after dinner we all three walked to Chawton Park, meaning to go into it, but it was too dirty, and we were obliged to keep on the outside. Mr. Tilson admired the trees very much, but grieved that they should not be turned into money . . .

On Monday I had the pleasure of receiving, unpacking and approving our Wedgwood ware. It all came very safely, and upon the whole is a good match, tho' I think they might have allowed us rather larger leaves, especially in such a year of fine foliage as this. One is apt to suppose that the woods about Birmingham must be blighted . . .

We began peas on Sunday, but our gatherings are very small not at all like the gathering in the Lady of the Lake. Yesterday I had the agreeable surprise of finding several scarlet strawberries quite ripe; had *you* been at home, this would have been a pleasure lost . . .

I had just left off writing and put on my things for walking to Alton, when Anna and her friend Harriot called in their way thither, so we went together. Their business was to provide

BELOW *A strawberry plant illustrated by Curtis in his* Botanical Magazine. *Mrs. Austen grew strawberries in the Chawton garden.*

ABOVE *Wedgwood's showroom in York Street. In 1813 Edward Knight and his daughter Fanny ordered a Wedgwood dinner service, part of which is in the Chawton Cottage dining room.*

BELOW *Original patterns for borders of Wedgwood china.*

mourning, against the King's death; and my mother has had a bombasine bought for her. I am not sorry to be back again, for the young ladies had a great deal to do – and without much method in doing it . . .

With love to you all,

Yrs. affecly. *J. A.*

The 'gathering in the Lady of the Lake': Sir Walter Scott's poem had been published the previous year, and Canto Three: The Gathering *is full of bloody revenge, anguish and sacrifice. Mrs. Austen wrote cannily that she had bought a bombasine 'thinking I should get it cheaper than when the poor King was actually dead'. This was somewhat premature: he lived until January 1820.*

CHAWTON SUNDAY EVENG. JANY 24 [1813]

My dear Cassandra

*T*HIS IS EXACTLY THE weather we could wish for, if you are but well enough to enjoy it . . .

Our party on Wednesday was not unagreeable, tho' as usual we wanted a better master of the house, one less anxious and fidgety, and more conversable. In consequence of a civil note that morng. from Mrs. Clement, I went with her and her husband in their tax cart; civility on both sides . . .

I could see nothing very promising between Mr. P. and Miss P. T. She placed herself on one side of him at first, but Miss Benn obliged her to move up higher; and she had an empty plate and even asked him to give her some mutton without being attended to for some time. There might be design in this . . . on his side; he might think an empty stomach the most favourable for love . . .

BELOW *'Butcher', a plate from* Costume of Great Britain *by* W. H. Pyne, *1808.*

As soon as a whist party was formed and a round table threatened, I made my mother an excuse, and came away; leaving just as many for *their* round table, as there were at Mrs. Grant's. I wish they might be as agreeable a set . . .

I have walked once to Alton and yesterday Miss Papillon and I walked together to call on the Garnets. *I* had a very agreeable walk and if she had not, more shame for her, for I was quite as entertaining as she was. Dame G. is pretty well, and we found her surrounded by her well-behaved, healthy, large-eyed children. I took her an old shift and promised her a set of our linen, and my companion left some of her bank stock with her . . .

I had fancied that Martha wd. be at Barton from last Saturday, but am best pleased to be mistaken. I hope she is now quite well. Tell her that I hunt away the rogues every night from under her bed; they feel the difference of her being gone.

Miss Benn, an impecunious Chawton neighbour, was treated by the Austen sisters with kindness and consideration. Mr. Papillon was the master of the house found wanting as host at the party. 'Mr. P. and Miss P. T.' were Mr. Papillon and Miss Terry. The 'tax-cart' was a two-wheeled cart, mainly used for trade or agricultural purposes and consequently taxed at a reduced rate. 'Mrs. Grant's': the reference is to the game of Speculation played at the Grants' party in Mansfield Park.

CHAWTON, FRIDAY JANUARY 29 [1813]

I HOPE YOU RECEIVED MY little parcel . . . on Wednesday eveng. my dear Cassandra, and that you will be ready to hear from me again on Sunday, for I feel that I must write to you today . . .

I want to tell you that I have got my own darling child from London, on Wednesday I received one copy, sent down by Falknor, with three lines from Henry to say that he had given

ABOVE AND BELOW *Cottagers from* Pyne's Microcosm, *1806. The class to which the Austens belonged accepted the care of the neighbouring poor as a matter of course.*

BELOW *West front of Chawton House, known as the Great House in order to differentiate it from Chawton Cottage.*

another to Charles and sent a 3d by the coach to Godmersham, just the two sets which I was least eager for the disposal of. I wrote to him immediately to beg for my two other sets . . . I shall write to Frank, that he may not think himself neglected . . .

Miss Benn dined with us on the very day of the book's coming, and in the eveng. we set fairly at it and read half the 1st vol. to her – prefacing that having intelligence from Henry that such a work wd. soon appear we had desired him to send it whenever it came out – and I believe it passed with her unsuspected. She was amused, poor soul! *That* she cd. not help – you know, with two such people to lead the way; but she really does seem to admire Elizabeth. I must confess that *I* think her as delightful a creature as ever appeared in print, and how I shall be able to tolerate those who do not like *her* at least, I do not know. There are a few typical errors – and a 'said he,' or a 'said she,' would sometimes make the dialogue more immediately clear – but

> 'I do not write for such dull elves
> As have not a great deal of ingenuity themselves.'

I am glad to find your enquiries have ended so well. If you cd. discover whether Northamptonshire is a country of hedgerows, I shd. be glad again.

We admire your charades excessively, but as yet have guessed only the 1st. The others seem very difficult. There is so much beauty in the versification however, that the finding them out is but a secondary pleasure.

The reference to 'my own darling child' was to the first copy of Pride and Prejudice. *Jane was anxious to preserve her incognito and was therefore pleased that 'it passed with her unsuspected'. The title page said 'By the Author of* Sense and Sensibility', *and this latter had simply been described as 'By a Lady'. 'I do not write for such dull elves': Jane was misquoting Scott's* Marmion.

"The sounds were retreating, and Anne distinguished no more. Her own emotions still kept her fixed. She had much to recover from, before she could move. The listener's proverbial fate was not absolutely hers; she had heard no evil of herself, but she had heard a great deal of very painful import. She saw how her own character was considered by Captain Wentworth; and there had been just that degree of feeling and curiosity about her in his manner, which must give her extreme agitation."

PERSUASION

CHAWTON THURSDAY FEB. 4 [1813]

My dear Cassandra

*Y*OUR LETTER WAS TRULY welcome and I am much obliged to you for all your praise; it came at a right time, for I had had some fits of disgust. Our 2d evening's reading to Miss Benn had not pleased me so well, but I believe something must be attributed to my mother's too rapid way of getting on; tho' she perfectly understands the characters herself, she cannot speak as they ought. Upon the whole however I am . . . well satisfied enough.

The work is rather too light and bright and sparkling; it wants shade; it wants to be stretched out here and there with a long chapter – of sense if it could be had; if not, of solemn specious nonsense – about something unconnected with the story; an essay on writing, a critique on Walter Scott, or the history of Buonaparté, or anything that would form a contrast, and bring the reader with increased delight to the playfulness and epigrammatism of the general style. I doubt your quite agreeing with me here – I know your starched notions . . .

Anne Elliot inadvertently overhears a conversation between Captain Wentworth (whom she loves) and Louisa Musgrove. She is distressed by what she hears.

LEFT *A fashion plate from Ackermann's* Repository *for July 1815 showing a lady at an exhibition.*

Thomas was married on Saturday, the wedding was kept at Neatham and that is all I know about it. Browning is quite a new broom and at present has no fault. He had lost some of his knowledge of waiting, and is I think rather slow, but he is not noisy, and not at all above being taught.

Thomas and Browning were, respectively, the outgoing and incoming Chawton manservants.

SLOANE ST. MONDAY MAY 24 [1813]

My dearest Cassandra

I AM VERY MUCH OBLIGED to you for writing to me . . . Your letter came just in time to save my going to Remnant's, and fit me for Christian's, where I bought Fanny's dimity . . .

Henry and I went to the exhibition in Spring Gardens. It is not thought a good collection, but I was very well pleased, particularly (pray tell Fanny) with a small portrait of Mrs. Bingley, excessively like her.

I went in hopes of seeing one of her sister, but there was no Mrs. Darcy; perhaps however, I may find her in the Great Exhibition which we shall go to, if we have time; I have no chance of her in the collection of Sir Joshua Reynolds's paintings which is now shewing in Pall Mall, and which we are also to visit.

Mrs. Bingley's is exactly herself, size, shaped face, features and sweetness; there never was a greater likeness. She is dressed in a white gown, with green ornaments, which convinces me of what I had always supposed, that green was a favourite colour with her. I dare say Mrs. D. will be in yellow . . .

I should like to see Miss Burdett very well, but that I am rather frightened by hearing that she wishes to be introduced to *me*. If I *am* a wild beast, I cannot help it. It is not my own fault . . .

ABOVE *A coloured engraving of an exhibition at Somerset House by Cruikshank. Jane wrote of a similar exhibition,* 'My preference for men and women, always inclines me to attend more to the company than the sight.'

ABOVE *A drawing by George Scharf of the backs of houses in Sloane Street showing the pleasant leafy gardens.*

Monday Eveng. We have been both to the exhibition and Sir J. Reynolds', and I am disappointed, for there was nothing like Mrs. D. at either. I can only imagine that Mr. D. prizes any picture of her too much to like it should be exposed to the public eye. I can imagine he wd. have that sort of feeling – that mixture of love, pride and delicacy.

Setting aside this disappointment, I had great amusement among the pictures; and the driving about, the carriage being open, was very pleasant. I liked my solitary elegance very much, and was ready to laugh all the time at my being where I was. I could not but feel that I had naturally small right to be parading about London in a barouche . . .

Yrs affecly. *J. Austen*

Mr. Darcy contemplates the idea of a portrait of Elizabeth Bennet.

66 'Have you any thing else to propose for my domestic felicity?'

'Oh! Yes. Do let the portraits of your uncle and aunt Philips be placed in the gallery at Pemberley. Put them next to your great uncle the judge. They are in the same profession, you know; only in different lines. As for your Elizabeth's picture, you must not attempt to have it taken, for what painter could do justice to those beautiful eyes?'

'It would not be easy, indeed, to catch their expression, but their colour and shape, and the eye-lashes, so remarkably fine, might be copied.'

At that moment they were met from another walk, by Mrs. Hurst and Elizabeth herself.

'I did not know that you intended to walk,' said Miss Bingley, in some confusion, lest they had been overheard. 99

PRIDE AND PREJUDICE

66In the gallery there were many family portraits, but they could have little to fix the attention of a stranger. Elizabeth walked on in quest of the only face whose features would be known to her. At last it arrested her — and she beheld a striking resemblance of Mr. Darcy, with such a smile over the face, as she remembered to have sometimes seen, when he looked at her. She stood several minutes before the picture in earnest contemplation, and returned to it again before they quitted the gallery.**99**

PRIDE AND PREJUDICE

Elizabeth herself is drawn to a portrait of Darcy at Pemberley.

To Francis Austen

CHAWTON JULY 3 [1813]

My dearest Frank

*B*EHOLD ME GOING TO write you as handsome a letter as I can! Wish me good luck. We have had the pleasure of hearing from you lately through Mary, who sent us some of the particulars of yours of June 18th (I think), written off Rugen, and we enter into the delight of your having so good a pilot. Why are you like Queen Elizth.? Because you know how to chuse wise ministers. Does not this prove you as great a captain as she was a queen? This may serve as a riddle for you to put forth among your officers, by way of increasing your proper consequence. It must be a real enjoyment to you, since you are obliged to leave England, to be where you are, seeing something of a new country and one that has been so distinguished as Sweden. You must have great pleasure in it. I hope you may have gone to Carlscroon. Your profession has its douceurs to recompense for some of its

ABOVE *Design for an open carriage from Felton's* Treatise on Carriages, *described as 'a carriage in form of a coach, the upper part may be opened at pleasure for the advantage of air and prospect in summer time'. A conveyance similar to Henry's barouche, so much enjoyed by Jane.*

BELOW *Children playing with a new doll, watercolour by E. F. Burney. Jane wrote of one little niece sending her love to another and promising her 'a doll the next time she goes to Godmersham'.*

RIGHT *Messrs. Lackington Allen & Co., booksellers at the Temple of Muses, Finsbury Square.*

privations; to an enquiring and observing mind like yours, such douceurs must be considerable. Gustavus Vasa, and Charles 12th, and Christiana and Linnaeus – do their ghosts rise up before you? I have a great respect for former Sweden. So zealous as it was for Protestantism! And I have always fancied it more like England than many countries; and according to the map, many of the names have a strong resemblance to the English.

We are in hopes of another visit from our true lawful Henry very soon, he is to be *our* guest this time. He is quite well I am happy to say, and does not leave it to *my* pen I am sure to communicate to you the joyful news of his being *Deputy* Receiver no longer. It is a promotion which he thoroughly enjoys; as well he may; the work of his own mind . . .

Upon the whole his spirits are very much recovered. If I may so express myself, his mind is not a mind for affliction. He is too busy, too active, too sanguine. Sincerely as he was attached to poor Eliza moreover . . . he was always so used to be away from her at times . . . especially when all the circumstances of her long and dreadful illness are taken into the account. He very long knew that she must die, and it was indeed a release at last.

Our mourning for her is not over, or we should be putting it on again for Mr. Thos. Leigh, the respectable, worthy, clever, agreeable Mr. Tho. Leigh, who has just closed a good life at the age of seventy-nine, and must have died the possessor of one of the finest estates in England and of more worthless nephews and nieces than any other private man in the United Kingdoms . . .

Charles's little girls were with us about a month, and had so endeared themselves that we were quite sorry to have them go. We have the pleasure however of hearing that they are thought very much improved at home – Harriet in health, Cassy in manners. Harriet is a truly sweet-tempered little darling . . .

I wonder whether you happened to see Mr. Blackall's marriage in the papers last Janry. We did. He was married at Clifton to a Miss Lewis whose father had been late of Antigua. I should very

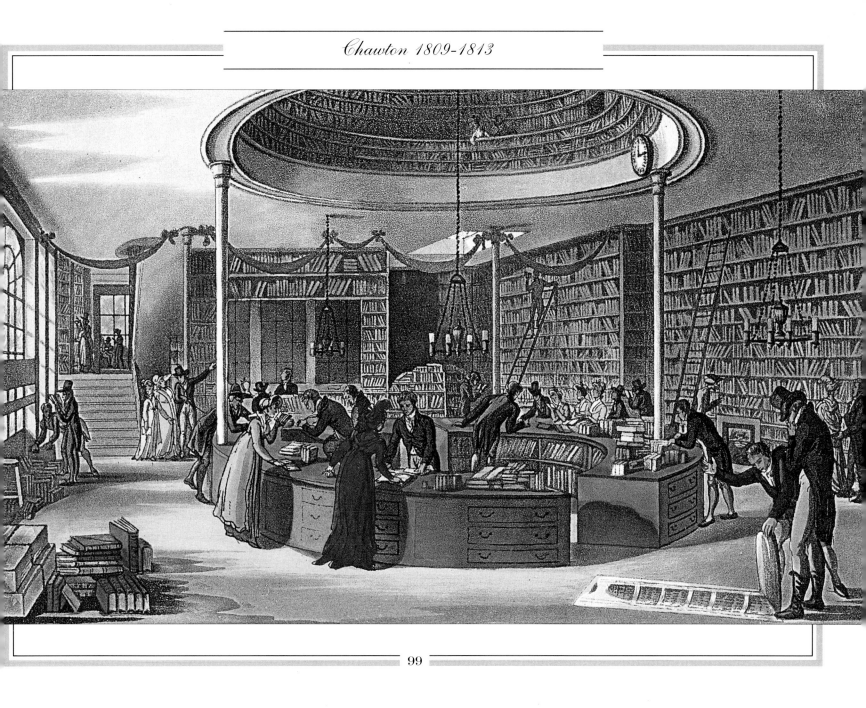

much like to know what sort of a woman she is. He was a piece of perfection, noisy perfection himself which I always recollect with regard. We had noticed a few months before his succeeding to a college living, the very living which we recollected his talking of and wishing for; an exceeding good one, Great Cadbury in Somersetshire. I would wish Miss Lewis to be of a silent turn and rather ignorant, but naturally intelligent and wishing to learn; fond of cold veal pies, green tea in the afternoon, and a green window blind at night.

July 6. God bless you. I hope you continue beautiful and brush your hair, but not all off.

We join in an infinity of love.

Yrs very affecly. *Jane Austen*

You will be glad to hear that every copy of S. and S. is sold, and that it has brought me £140 besides the copyright, if that shd. ever be of any value. I have now, therefore, written myself into £250 which only makes me long for more. I have something in hand which I hope on the credit of P. and P. will sell well, tho' not half so entertaining. And by the by – shall you object to my

RIGHT *Lake Windermere, an aquatint from William Gilpin's* Observations Relative to Picturesque Beauty, *epitomising the ideals of Romantic beauty, which, to Jane's disappointment, were ignored by her nephew Edward on a northern tour.*

mentioning the Elephant in it, and two or three other of your old ships? I *have* done it, but it shall not stay, to make you angry. They are only just mentioned.

Henry was now Receiver General, no longer Deputy Receiver, for Oxfordshire. His spirits were 'very much recovered' from Eliza's death on 25 April. Mr. Blackall was Jane's bombastic suitor mentioned on 17 November 1798. The 'something in hand' was Mansfield Park.

To Francis Austen

GODMERSHAM PARK SEPT: 25 [1813]

My dearest Frank

*T*HE 11TH OF THIS MONTH brought me your letter and I assure you I thought it very well worth its 2s/3d . . .

We left Chawton on the 14th, spent two entire days in town and arrived here on ye 17th. My br., Fanny, Lizzy, Marianne and I composed this division of the family, and filled his carriage, inside and out. Two post-chaises, under the escort of George conveyed eight more across the country, the chair brought two, two others came on horseback, and the rest by the coach – and so by one means or another we all are removed. It puts me in mind of the account of St. Paul's shipwreck, where all are said by different means to reach the shore in safety.

I expect to be here about two months. Edward is to be in Hampshire again in November and will take me back . . .

Henry has probably sent you his own account of his visit in Scotland. I wish he had had more time and could have gone further north, and deviated to the Lakes in his way back; but what he was able to do seems to have afforded him great

ABOVE AND RIGHT *A chair-back gig and a travelling post-chaise, from Felton's* Treatise on Carriages, *of the types used by the unwieldy Godmersham party on their journey home from London.*

enjoyment and he met with scenes of higher beauty in Roxburghshire than I had supposed the South of Scotland possessed. Our nephew's gratification was less keen than our brother's. Edward is no enthusiast in the beauties of Nature. His enthusiasm is for the sports of the field only. He is a very promising and pleasing young man however upon the whole, behaves with great propriety to his father and great kindness to his brothers and sisters – and we must forgive his thinking more of grouse and partridges than lakes and mountains . . .

In this house there is a constant succession of small events, somebody is always going or coming; this morng. we had Edwd. Bridges unexpectedly to breakfast with us, in his way from Ramsgate where is his wife, to Lenham where is his church and tomorrow he dines and sleeps here on his return. They have been all the summer at Ramsgate for *her* health; she is a poor honey – the sort of woman who gives me the idea of being determined never to be well and who likes her spasms and nervousness and the consequence they give her, better than anything else. This is an ill natured statement to send all over the Baltic! . . . Mr. Sherer is quite a new Mr. Sherer to me; I heard him for the first time last Sunday, and he gave us an excellent sermon – a little too eager sometimes in his delivery, but that is to me a better extreme than the want of animation, especially when it evidently comes from the heart as in him . . .

I thank you very warmly for your kind consent to my application and the kind hint which followed it. I was previously aware of what I shd. be laying myself open to but the truth is that the secret has spread so far as to be scarcely the shadow of a secret now and that I believe whenever the 3d appears, I shall not even attempt to tell lies about it. I shall rather try to make all the money than all the mystery I can of it. People shall pay for their knowledge if I can make them . . .

I take it for granted that Mary has told you of Anna's engagement to Ben Lefroy. It came upon us without much preparation;

RIGHT *'Rabbit Shooting', a coloured aquatint after a drawing by Samuel Howitt.*

at the same time, there was that about her which kept us in a constant preparation for something. We are anxious to have it go on well, there being quite as much in his favour as the chances are likely to give her in any matrimonial connection. I believe he is sensible, certainly very religious, well connected, and with some independence. There is an unfortunate dissimilarity of taste between them in one respect which gives us some apprehensions, he hates company and she is very fond of it; this, with some queerness of temper on his side and much unsteadiness on hers, is untoward. I hope Edward's family visit to Chawton will be yearly . . .

I remain

Your very affecte. Sister *J. Austen*

GODMERSHAM PARK MONDAY OCT. 11 [1813]

ABOVE *'Foxhunting – The Chase'*, a coloured aquatint after a drawing by Samuel Howitt.

You WILL HAVE EDWARD'S letter tomorrow. He tells me that he did not send you any news to interfere with mine, but I do not think there is much for anybody to send at present . . .

As I wrote of my nephews with a little bitterness in my last, I think it particularly incumbent on me to do them justice now, and I have great pleasure in saying that they were both at the Sacrament yesterday. After having much praised or much blamed anybody, one is generally sensible of something just the reverse soon afterwards. Now these two boys who are out with the foxhounds will come home and disgust me again by some habit of luxury or some proof of sporting mania – unless I keep it off by this prediction. They amuse themselves very comfortably in the eveng. by netting; they are each about a rabbit net, and sit as deedily to it, side by side, as any two Uncle Franks could do . . .

Tuesday . . . Dear Mrs. Digweed! I cannot bear that she shd. not be foolishly happy after a ball . . .

My brother desires his best love and thanks for all your information . . . Have you any idea of returning with him to Henrietta St. and finishing your visit then? Tell me your sweet little innocent ideas . . .

Yrs. very affecly. *J. Austen*

GODMERSHAM PARK THURSDAY OCT. 14 [1813]

My dearest Cassandra

*N*OW I WILL PREPARE FOR Mr. Lushington, and as it will be wisest also to prepare for his not coming or my not getting a frank I shall write very close from the first and even leave room for the seal in the proper place . . .

A letter from Wrotham yesterday, offering an early visit here; and Mr. and Mrs. Moore and one child are to come on Monday for 10 days. I hope Charles and Fanny may not fix the same time – but if they come at all in October they *must*. What is the use of hoping? The two parties of children is the chief evil.

To be sure, here we are, the very thing has happened, or rather worse, a letter from Charles this very morng. which gives us reason to suppose they may come here today . . .

By her own desire *Mrs.* Fanny is to be put in the room next the nursery, her baby in a little bed by her; and as Cassy is to have the closet within and Betsey William's little hole they will be all very snug together. I shall be most happy to see dear Charles, and he will be as happy as he can with a cross child, or some such care pressing on him at the time . . .

The comfort of the billiard table here is very great. It draws all the gentlemen to it whenever they are within, especially after dinner, so that my Br., Fanny and I have the library to ourselves in delightful quiet . . .

BELOW '*Ramsgate Harbour*' by *Thomas Rowlandson. Jane speaks of Mrs. Edward Bridges spending the summer at Ramsgate for her health.*

Friday. They came last night at about 7. We had given them up, but *I still* expected them to come ... They had a very rough passage, he wd. not have ventured if he had known how bad it wd. be.

However, here they are safe and well, just like their own nice selves, Fanny looking as neat and white this morng. as possible, and dear Charles all affectionate, placid, quiet, cheerful good humour. They are both looking very well, but poor little Cassy is grown extremely thin and looks poorly. I hope a week's country air and exercise may do her good ...

It was quite an eveng. of confusion as you may suppose — at first we were all walking about from one part of the house to the other — then came a fresh dinner in the breakfast room for Charles and his wife, which Fanny and I attended — then we moved into the library, were joined by the dining room people, were introduced and so forth — and then we had tea and coffee which was not over till past 10. Billiards again drew all the odd ones away, and Edwd., Charles, the two Fannys and I sat snugly talking. I shall be glad to have our numbers a little reduced, and by the time you receive this we shall be only a family, tho' a large family party. Mr. Lushington goes tomorrow.

Now I must speak of *him* — and I like him very much. I am sure he is clever and a man of taste. He got a vol. of Milton last night and spoke of it with warmth. He is quite an M.P. — very smiling, with an exceeding good address, and readiness of language. I am rather in love with him. I dare say he is ambitious and insincere ...

Yours very affecly. *J. Austen*

Stephen Lushington of Norton Court, Kent, was the Member of Parliament for Canterbury. For reasons of economy Charles had taken his wife and children to live on board the Namur *off Sheerness, where he was on patrol duty.*

BELOW *Tea was a welcome diversion due to the long gap after the early dinner hour of the time, and was sometimes accompanied by a tray of more solid eatables.*

CHAWTON 1813–1816

• ● •

Years of Fulfilment and Acclaim

The following group of Jane Austen's letters begins with the novelist enjoying the luxury of her visit to Godmersham. With her thirty-eighth birthday looming, she had begun to contemplate middle age: 'By the by, as I must leave off being young, I find many douceurs in being a sort of chaperone for I am put on the sofa near the fire and can drink as much wine as I like.' Her central preoccupations seem now to have shifted away from herself and towards a greater affectionate relationship with the next generation. Two years later she was to write to her ten-year-old niece Caroline congratulating her on becoming an aunt: 'I have always maintained the importance of aunts as much as possible'; and it was a role in which she herself excelled.

There are among these letters some delightful ones written to two of her nieces. Unlike the rest of the correspondence, which is to a great extent the objective chronicling of daily happenings, these letters are devoted almost exclusively to a consideration of single topics, with a consequent gain in intensity and a sense of intimacy. To her favourite Fanny Knight, Jane wrote with affectionate tact and care about the problems of Fanny's love affairs; and Anna Austen, having sent the manuscript of a novel for her aunt to criticise, was the fortunate recipient of long detailed comments on novel writing. These are fascinating now for what they tell of Jane Austen's methods of composition, of selection, and of that infinite capacity for taking pains said to characterise

RIGHT *Map of Hans Place, where Henry had his last London house. A detail from* A Plan of the Cities of London and Westminster, *1799, showing the adjoining surprisingly rural nursery gardens.*

genius. Every detail had to be exact and convincing in order to produce that sense of reality she so triumphantly achieved in her own work. It was, she warned Anna, of the greatest importance never to stray outside the field of one's own knowledge. 'Let the Portmans go to Ireland', she advised on 10 August 1814, 'but as you know nothing of the manners there, you had better not go with them. You will be in danger of giving false representations.' And in the letter of 9 September of the same year came the famous remark: 'You are now collecting your people delightfully, getting them exactly into such a spot as is the delight of my life; 3 or 4 families in a country village is the very thing to work on.' It is interesting to reflect that Jane's two privileged young correspondents were the same age she herself had been when her letters began in 1796: at Fanny's age she was flirting with Tom Lefroy; at Anna's she had already completed the first versions of *Sense and Sensibility* and *Pride and Prejudice*.

Jane's own work meanwhile continued to prosper: *Mansfield Park* was accepted for publication during the autumn of 1813, and in the New Year she began to write *Emma*. In March 1814 Henry took her to stay with him in London, and read *Mansfield Park* (presumably in manuscript or proof) during their journey. Jane was pleased with his favourable comments. The novel was published in May, and the first edition was sold out by November, despite a lack of reviews.

During the summer Jane was again in London, staying at 23 Hans Place, Henry's new house. Recovered from the loss of his wife, Henry was enjoying a flirtatious time as a desirable widower, rich and attractive. Jane's account of his harem of ladies was unenthusiastic.

On 31 August Fanny, Charles's wife, died after the birth of her fourth child, leaving Charles to care for three small daughters. In November Anna was married to Benjamin Lefroy at Steventon. Their first home was at Hendon, but within a year they had moved to Wyards, near Chawton, close to Anna's aunts.

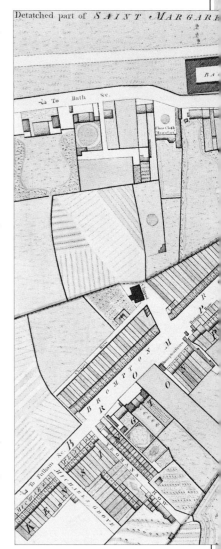

Emma was finished in March 1815 and published by John Murray at the end of the year. 'He is a rogue of course,' Jane wrote to Cassandra, 'but a civil one.' She was to find him affable and helpful, and he pleased her with generous loans of books.

During the summer of 1815 work began on *Persuasion*, and by the autumn Jane was again in London for a visit which was prolonged whilst she nursed Henry through a sudden and alarming illness. On his recovery Jane was introduced by one of her brother's doctors to James Stanier Clarke, librarian and domestic chaplain to the Prince Regent. Mr. Clarke spoke of the Prince's admiration for her work, and his wish that she should be conducted round Carlton House. Jane strongly disapproved of the Prince's luxurious excesses, and made her visit with ambivalent feelings. Stanier Clarke suggested that it would be a graceful gesture if she were to dedicate her next work to the Prince. The whole episode was somewhat tiresome for her, and she worried over the exact form of the dedication; but a specially bound set of *Emma* in red morocco gilt was presently delivered to Carlton House.

This odd encounter was still not quite finished, Clarke writing several times during the next months making wildly inappropriate suggestions for further novels, designed to reflect on aspects of his own career. One was to be about a clergyman sent to sea 'as the friend of some distinguished naval chaplain about a court — you can then bring forward like Le Sage many interesting scenes of character and interest'; another was for an 'historical romance, illustrative of the history of the august House of Coburg'. Jane's replies (11 December 1815 and 1 April 1816) were polite, but with a tinge of mockery.

London, after Henry's return to health, was agreeable; Jane enjoyed small parties in company with Fanny Knight, who had by now joined the Hans Place party, and amused her aunt by indulging in mild love affairs. The two were happy together: 'Aunt Jane and I very snug' Fanny recorded.

BELOW *The grand façade of the Prince Regent's Carlton House, a print from Pyne's* Royal Residences.

BELOW *Miniature of Henry Austen as a curate. During Jane's last years he assisted Mr. Papillon, the rector of Chawton.*

RIGHT *Chilham Castle, home of James Wildman, from J. G. Wood's* Views of the Noblemen's and Gentlemen's Seats of Kent, *1800.*

Before Christmas Jane returned to Chawton, and 1816 began with the good reception of *Emma*. She was particularly pleased by Walter Scott's (unsigned) article in the prestigious *Quarterly Review*. It is sad that she did not live to enjoy his diary entry for 14 March 1826: 'Read again, for the third time at least, Miss Austen's finely written novel of *Pride and Prejudice*. That young lady had a talent for describing the involvements and feelings and characters of ordinary life, which is to me the most wonderful I ever met with. The big Bow-Wow strain I can do myself like any now going; but the exquisite touch which renders ordinary common-place things and characters interesting from the truth of the description and the sentiment is denied to me.'

On 15 March Henry's banking business failed, involving the Austens in financial difficulty. For most men this disaster would have had lasting effects, but Henry's temperament was so optimistic that he was able to shrug off his losses, and to revert to his youthful ambition of ordination into the Church of England. By the end of the year he was appointed curate at Chawton – a happy outcome for Jane. She found it difficult, however, to match her brother's resilience, and the shock left its mark on her. She felt tired and depressed: sinister portents of what was to come.

GODMERSHAM PARK SATURDAY NOV. 6 [1813]

My dearest Cassandra

*H*AVING HALF AN HOUR before breakfast – (very snug, in my own room, lovely morng., excellent fire, fancy me) I will give you some account of the last two days. And yet, what is there to be told? I shall get foolishly minute unless I cut the matter short.

We met only the Brittons at Chilham Castle, besides a Mr. and Mrs. Osborne and a Miss Lee staying in the house, and were only 14 altogether . . .

By the by, as I must leave off being young, I find many douceurs in being a sort of chaperone for I am put on the sofa near the fire and can drink as much wine as I like. We had music in the eveng., Fanny and Miss Wildman played, and Mr. James Wildman sat close by and listened, or pretended to listen . . . We had a beautiful night for our frisks . . .

When the concert was over, Mrs. Harrison and I found each other out and had a very comfortable little complimentary friendly chat. She is a sweet woman, still quite a sweet woman in herself, and so like her sister! I could almost have thought I was speaking to Mrs. Lefroy . . .

Since I wrote last, my 2d edit. has stared me in the face. Mary tells me that Eliza means to buy it. I wish she may . . . I cannot help hoping that *many* will feel themselves obliged to buy it. I shall not mind imagining it a disagreeable duty to them, so as they do it.

You shall hear from me once more, some day or other.

Yours very affec:ly *J.A.*

Chilham Castle near Godmersham belonged to Mr. James Wildman, an admirer of Fanny Knight's. Mrs. Charlotte Harrison was the sister of Jane's much-mourned friend, Mrs. Lefroy.

BELOW *A group singing round the piano by candlelight.*

HENRIETTA ST. WEDNESDAY MARCH 2 [1814]

My dear Cassandra

*Y*OU WERE WRONG IN thinking of us at Guildford last night, we were at Cobham.

We did not begin reading till Bentley Green. Henry's approbation is hitherto even equal to my wishes; he says it is very

ABOVE *An early nineteenth-century view of travellers arriving at Kingston, a major staging post, drawn by Thomas Rowlandson.*

different from the other two, but does not appear to think it at all inferior . . . I am afraid he has gone through the most entertaining part. He took to Lady B. and Mrs. N. most kindly, and gives great praise to the drawing of the characters. He understands them all, likes Fanny and I think foresees how it will all be.

We went to bed at 10. I was very tired, but slept to a miracle and am lovely today, and at present Henry seems to have no complaint. We left Cobham at ½ past 8; stopped to bait and breakfast at Kingston and were in this house considerably before 2 – quite in the style of Mr. Knight. Nice smiling Mr. Barlowe met us at the door, and in reply to enquiries after news, said that peace was generally expected . . . We had some snow storms yesterday, and a smart frost at night – which gave us a hard road from Cobham to Kingston; but as it was then getting dirty and heavy, Henry had a pair of leaders put on from the latter place to the bottom of Sloane St . . . I watched for *veils* as we drove through the streets, and had the pleasure of seeing several upon vulgar heads . . .

Places are secured at Drury Lane for Saturday, but so great is the rage for seeing Kean that only a 3d and 4th row could be got; as it is in a front box however, I hope we shall do pretty well. Shylock. A good play for Fanny . . .

It is eveng. We have drank tea and I have torn through the 3d vol. of the Heroine. I do not think it falls off. It is a delightful burlesque, particularly on the Radcliffe style. Henry is going on with Mansfield Park; He admires H. Crawford – I mean properly, as a clever, pleasant man. I tell you all the good I can . . .

Yours affecly. *J. Austen*

Henry was reading Mansfield Park *in proof and it was to this that he gave his approbation. The Heroine was by E. S. Barrett. Mrs. Radcliffe was the doyenne of the Gothick horror novel. Her* Mysteries of Udolpho *was much admired by Catherine Morland in* Northanger Abbey.

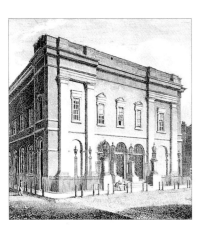

ABOVE AND RIGHT *Theatre Royal, Drury Lane, an engraving of the exterior and the interior drawn and etched by Rowlandson for Ackermann in 1814. 'Places are secured at Drury Lane for Saturday, but so great is the rage for seeing Kean that only a 3d and 4th row could be got; as it is in a front box however, I hope we shall do pretty well. Shylock. A good play for Fanny.'*

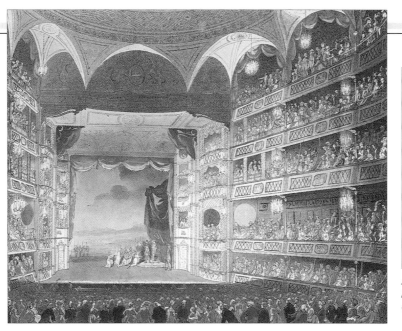

ABOVE *'Mr Kean in the character of Shylock.' 'We were quite satisfied with Kean,' wrote Jane.*

Catherine Morland and her false friend Isabella share the thrills of the Gothick horror novel.

66 'But, my dearest Catherine, what have you been doing with yourself all this morning? Have you gone on with Udolpho?'

'Yes, I have been reading it ever since I woke; and I am got to the black veil . . . Oh! I am delighted with the book! I should like to spend my whole life in reading it. I assure you, if it had not been to meet you, I would not have come away from it for all the world.'

'Dear creature! how much I am obliged to you; and when you have finished Udolpho, we will read the Italian together; and I have made out a list of ten or twelve more of the same kind for you . . . Those will last us some time.'

'Yes, pretty well; but are they all horrid, are you sure they are all horrid?' 99

NORTHANGER ABBEY

BELOW *'The Indian Jugglers' as they appeared in Ackermann's* Repository *which stated that 'Perhaps there is not a country in the world where every species of curious novelty meets with such certain encouragements as in England.'*

HENRIETTA ST. WEDNESDAY MARCH 9 [1814]

WELL, WE WENT TO THE play again last night, and as we were out great part of the morning too, shopping and seeing the Indian jugglers, I am very glad to be quiet now till dressing time . . .

The Farmer's Wife is a musical thing in 3 acts, and as Edward was steady in not staying for anything more, we were at home before 10.

Fanny and Mr. J. P. are delighted with Miss S., and her merit in singing is I dare say very great; that she gave *me* no pleasure is no reflection upon her, nor I hope upon myself, being what nature made me on that article. All that I am sensible of in Miss S. is a pleasing person and no skill in acting . . .

I have a cold too as well as my mother and Martha. Let it be a generous emulation between us which can get rid of it first.

I wear my gauze gown today, long sleeves and all; I shall see how they succeed, but as yet I have no reason to suppose long sleeves are allowable. I have lowered the bosom especially at the corners, and plaited black satin ribbon round the top. Such will be my costume of vine leaves and paste . . .

What cruel weather this is! And here is Lord Portsmouth married too to Miss Hanson!

Henry has finished Mansfield Park, and his approbation has not lessened. He found the last half of the last volume extremely interesting.

On Friday we are to be snug, with only Mr. Barlowe and an evening of business. I am so pleased that the mead is brewed! . . . If Cassandra has filled my bed with fleas, I am sure they must bite herself. I have written to Mrs. Hill and care for nobody.

Yours affecly. *J. Austen*

'Mr. J. P' was Mr. John Pemberton Plumtre.

BELOW *A long-sleeved gown from* Ackermann's Repository *for June 1814. 'I wear my gauze gown today, long sleeves and all; I shall see how they succeed, but as yet I have no reason to suppose long sleeves are allowable.'*

To Anna Austen

CHAWTON WEDNESDAY AUG 10 [1814]

My dear Anna

I AM QUITE ASHAMED TO find that I have never answered some questions of yours in a former note. I kept it on purpose to refer to it . . . and then forgot it. I like the name 'Which is the Heroine?' very well, and I dare say shall grow to like it very much in time – but 'Enthusiasm' was something so very superior that every common title must appear to disadvantage . . .

Wednesday 17. We have now just finished the 1st of the 3 books I had the pleasure of receiving yesterday; *I* read it aloud – and we are all very much amused, and like the work quite as well as ever . . .

My corrections have not been more important than before; here and there, we have thought the sense might be expressed in fewer words – and I have scratched out Sir Tho. from walking with the other men to the stables etc. the very day after breaking his arm – for though I find your papa *did* walk out immediately after *his* arm was set, I think it can be so little usual as to *appear* unnatural in a book. And it does not seem to be material that Sir Tho. should go with them. Lyme will not do. Lyme is towards 40 miles' distance from Dawlish and would not be talked of there . . .

I have also scratched out the introduction between Lord P. and his brother and Mr. Griffin. A country surgeon (don't tell Mr. C. Lyford) would not be introduced to men of their rank. And when Mr. Portman is first brought in, he wd. not be introduced as *the Honble. That* distinction is never mentioned at such times . . . Now, we have finished the 2d book, or rather the 5th I *do* think you had better omit Lady Helena's postscript; to those who are acquainted with P. and P. it will seem an imitation . . .

ABOVE *Cabinet writing table and chair as shown in Ackermann's* Repository *for January 1810, described as being of mahogany with rosewood, satinwood and kingwood and having private drawers in the writing part with ink and sandglasses, probably similar to Jane Austen's own.*

I am very much pleased with Egerton as yet. I did not expect to like him, but I do; and Susan is a very nice little animated creature – but St. Julian is the delight of one's life. He is quite interesting. The whole of his break-off with Lady H. is very well done. Yes, Russell Square is a very proper distance from Berkeley St. We are reading the last book . . .

Thursday. We finished it last night, after our return from drinking tea at the Gt. House. The last chapter does not please us quite so well, we do not thoroughly like *the play*; perhaps from having had too much of plays . . . And we think you had better not leave England. Let the Portmans go to Ireland, but as you know nothing of the manners there, you had better not go with them. You will be in danger of giving false representations . . .

I have not yet noticed St. Julian's serious conversation with Cecilia, but I liked it exceedingly; what he says about the madness of otherwise sensible women, on the subject of their daughters coming out, is worth its weight in gold . . .

Yours very affec:ly *J. Austen*

'Which is the Heroine?' was a new suggestion for the title of Anna's projected three-volume novel, which Jane Austen went on to discuss in some detail.

To Anna Austen

CHAWTON SEPT: 9 [1814]

My dear Anna

WE HAVE BEEN VERY much amused by your 3 books, but I have a good many criticisms to make more than you will like. We are not satisfied with Mrs. F.'s settling herself as tenant and near

ABOVE *The only full-face portrait of Jane Austen, c.1801, executed in pencil and watercolour by her sister Cassandra.*

neighbour to such a man as Sir T. H. without having some other inducement to go there; she ought to have some friend living thereabouts to tempt her. A woman, going with two girls just growing up, into a neighbourhood where she knows nobody, is an awkwardness which so prudent a woman as Mrs. F. would not be likely to fall into. Remember, she is very prudent; you must not let her act inconsistently. Give her a friend, and let that friend be invited to meet her at the Priory, and we shall have no objection to her dining there as she does; but otherwise, a woman in her situation would hardly go there, before she had been visited by other families . . .

Your G. M. is more disturbed at Mrs. F.'s not returning the Egertons' visit sooner than anything else. They ought to have called at the parsonage before Sunday. You describe a sweet place, but your descriptions are often more minute than will be liked. You give too many particulars of right hand and left. Mrs. F. is not careful enough of Susan's health; Susan ought not to be walking out so soon after heavy rains, taking long walks in the

RIGHT *'View of Ostree, near Faversham' in Kent, by Thomas Rowlandson. A country village scene of the kind recommended by Jane Austen when advising her niece to write from personal experience only.*

dirt. An anxious mother would not suffer it. I like your Susan very much indeed, she is a sweet creature, her playfulness of fancy is very delightful. I liked her as she is *now* exceedingly, but I am not so well satisfied with her behaviour to George R. At first she seemed all over attachment and feeling, and afterwards to have none at all; she is so extremely composed at the ball . . . She seems to have changed her character.

You are now collecting your people delightfully, getting them exactly into such a spot as is the delight of my life. 3 or 4 families in a country village is the very thing to work on . . .

I hope when you have written a great deal more you will be equal to scratching out some of the past. The scene with Mrs. Mellish, I should condemn; it is prosy and nothing to the purpose . . . the more you can find in your heart to curtail between Dawlish and Newton Priors, the better I think it will be. One does not care for girls till they are grown up.

I shall be very happy to receive more of your work, if more is ready; and you write so fast, that I have great hopes Mr. D. will come freighted back with such a cargo as not all his hops or his sheep could equal the value of . . .

Yrs. affec:ly *J. A*usten

Anna's 'G.M.' was her grandmother.

ABOVE *Diana Sperling's watercolour of walking to dinner through the mud, a practice deplored by Jane in her critique of her niece Anna's novel.*

To Anna Austen

CHAWTON WEDNESDAY SEPT: 28 [1814]

My dear Anna

I HOPE YOU DO NOT depend on having your book back again immediately. I kept it that your G. mama may hear it – for it

ABOVE AND BELOW *Engravings of Walter Scott and Maria Edgeworth.*

FAR RIGHT *A lady reading in morning dress from Ackermann's* Repository. *Jane Austen was regarded by her family as excelling at reading aloud.*

has not been possible yet to have any public reading. I have read it to your Aunt Cassandra however – in our own room at night, while we undressed – and with a great deal of pleaure. We like the first chapter extremely with only a little doubt whether Ly. Helena is not almost *too* foolish. The matrimonial dialogue is very good certainly. I like Susan as well as ever and begin now not to care at all about Cecilia; she may stay at Easton Court as long as she likes. Henry Mellish I am afraid will be too much in the common novel style – a handsome, amiable, unexceptional young man (such as do not much abound in real life) desperately in love, and all in vain . . .

Devereaux Forester's being ruined by his vanity is extremely good; but I wish you would not let him plunge into a 'vortex of dissipation'. I do not object to the thing, but I cannot bear the expression; it is such thorough novel slang – and so old, that I dare say Adam met with it in the first novel he opened . . .

Walter Scott has no business to write novels, especially good ones. It is not fair. He has fame and profit enough as a poet, and should not be taking the bread out of other people's mouths. I do not like him, and do not mean to like Waverley if I can help it – but fear I must . . . I have made up my mind to like no novels really but Miss Edgeworth's, yours and my own . . .

I am very fond of Sherlock's sermons, prefer them to almost any.

Your affecte. Aunt *J. Austen*

Sir Walter Scott's Waverley *had just been published. Scott shared Jane's admiration for Maria Edgeworth, the Irish writer, to whom Jane sent a copy of* Emma.

To Fanny Knight

CHAWTON FRIDAY NOV: 18 [1814]

BELOW *A demure portrait of Fanny Knight by her Aunt Cassandra.*

I FEEL QUITE AS DOUBTFUL as you could be my dearest Fanny, as to *when* my letter may be finished, for I can command very little quiet time at present, but yet I must begin, for I know you will be glad to hear as soon as possible, and I really am impatient myself – to be writing something on so very interesting a subject, though I have no hope of writing anything to the purpose. I shall do very little more I dare say than say over again, what you have said before.

I was certainly a good deal surprised *at first* – as I had no suspicion of any change in your feelings, and I have no scruple in saying that you cannot be in love. My dear Fanny, I am ready to laugh at the idea – and yet it is no laughing matter to have had you so mistaken as to your own feelings – and with all my heart I wish I had cautioned you on that point when first you spoke to me; but, tho' I did not think you then so *much* in love as you thought yourself, I did consider you as being attached in a degree – quite sufficiently for happiness, as I had no doubt it would increase with opportunity. And from the time of our being in London together, I thought you really very much in love. But you certainly are not at all – there is no concealing it.

What strange creatures we are! It seems as if your being secure of him (as you say yourself) had made you indifferent . . .

Poor dear Mr. J. P.! Oh! dear Fanny! Your mistake has been one that thousands of women fall into. He was the *first* young man who attached himself to you. That was the charm, and most powerful it is. Among the multitudes however that make the same mistake with yourself, there can be few indeed who have so little reason to regret it; *his* character and *his* attachment leave you nothing to be ashamed of.

Upon the whole, what is to be done? You certainly *have* encouraged him to such a point as to make him feel almost secure of you – you have no inclination for any other person. His situation in life, family, friends, and above all his character – his uncommonly amiable mind, strict principles, just notions, good habits, *all* that *you* know so well how to value, *all* that really is of the first importance – everything of this nature pleads his cause most strongly. You have no doubt of his having superior abilities – he has proved it at the university – he is I dare say such a scholar as your agreeable, idle brothers would ill bear a comparison with.

Oh! my dear Fanny, the more I write about him, the warmer my feelings become, the more strongly I feel the sterling worth of such a young man and the desirableness of your growing in love with him again. I recommend this most thoroughly. There *are* such beings in the world perhaps, one in a thousand, as the creature you and I should think perfection where grace and spirit are united to worth, where the manners are equal to the heart and understanding, but such a person may not come in your way, or if he does, he may not be the eldest son of a man of fortune, the brother of your particular friend, and belonging to your own country . . .

Think of all this Fanny. Mr. J. P. has advantages which do not often meet in one person. His only fault indeed seems modesty. If he were less modest, he would be more agreeable, speak louder, and look impudenter; and is not it a fine character of which modesty is the only defect? I have no doubt he will get more lively and more like yourselves as he is more with you; he will catch your ways if he belongs to you. And as to there being any objection from his *goodness*, from the danger of his becoming even evangelical, I cannot admit *that*. I am by no means convinced that we ought not all to be evangelicals, and am at least persuaded that they who are so from reason and feeling, must be happiest and safest. Do not be frightened from the connection by your brothers having most wit. Wisdom is better

BELOW *A scholar dressed as Fanny's 'Poor dear Mr. J. P.' would have been as an Oxford undergraduate, from Ackermann's* A History of the University of Oxford, *1814.*

than wit, and in the long run will certainly have the laugh on her side; and don't be frightened by the idea of his acting more strictly up to the precepts of the New Testament than others.

And now, my dear Fanny, having written so much on one side of the question, I shall turn round and entreat you not to commit yourself farther, and not to think of accepting him unless you really do like him. Anything is to be preferred or endured rather than marrying without affection; and if his deficiencies of manner etc. etc. strike you more than all his good qualities, if you continue to think strongly of them, give him up at once . . .

We have heard nothing fresh from Anna. I trust she is very comfortable in her new home. Her letters have been very sensible and satisfactory, with no *parade* of happiness, which I liked them the better for. I have often known young married women write in a way I did not like, in that respect.

You will be glad to hear that the first edit. of M. P. is all sold. Your Uncle Henry is rather wanting me to come to town, to settle about a 2d edit . . . I am very greedy and want to make the most of it, but as you are much above caring about money I shall not plague you with any particulars. The pleasures of vanity are more within your comprehension, and you will enter into mine, at receiving the *praise* which every now and then comes to me, through some channel or other . . .

Yours very affecly. *J. Austen*

Your trying to excite your own feelings by a visit to his room amused me excessively – the dirty shaving rag was exquisite! Such a circumstance ought to be in print. Much too good to be lost.

'We have heard nothing fresh from Anna' refers to Anna's recent marriage to Ben Lefroy, which had taken place on 8 November.

RIGHT *'Royal Mail Coach'. 'Protected by the coachman and guard, armed with a blunderbuss and brace of pistols each . . . The mail coaches are obliged to be very punctual to the time fixed at their different stages . . . these posts are made daily, instead of 3 days per week, to 320 towns.'*

ABOVE *A maid receiving the post, from Pyne's* World in Miniature.

ABOVE *Wyards, Ben and Anna Lefroy's house near Chawton, painted by Anna herself.*

BELOW AND FAR RIGHT *Two
Ackermann's* Repository *prints of
ball gowns such as a fashionable
lady might have worn in 1809.*

To Fanny Knight

23 HANS PLACE: WEDNESDAY NOV. 30 [1814]

I AM VERY MUCH OBLIGED to you my dear Fanny for your
letter, and I hope you will write again soon . . .

Now my dearest Fanny, I will begin a subject which comes in
very naturally. You frighten me out of my wits by your reference.
Your affection gives me the highest pleasure, but indeed you
must not let anything depend on my opinion. Your own feelings
and none but your own, should determine such an important
point. So far however as answering your question, I have no
scruple. I am perfectly convinced that your present feelings,
supposing you were to marry *now*, would be sufficient for his
happiness; but when I think how very, very far it is from a *now*,
and take everything that *may be* into consideration, I dare not
say, 'Determine to accept him.' The risk is too great for *you*,
unless your own sentiments prompt it.

You will think me perverse perhaps; in my last letter I was
urging everything in his favour, and now I am inclining the other
way; but I cannot help it; I am at present more impressed with
the possible evil that may arise to *you* from engaging yourself to
him – in word or mind – than with anything else. When I
consider how few young men you have yet seen much of, how
capable you are (yes, I do still think you *very* capable) of being
really in love and how full of temptation the next 6 or 7 years of
your life will probably be – (it is the very period of life for the
strongest attachments to be formed) – I cannot wish you with
your present very cool feelings to devote yourself in honour to
him. It is very true that you never may attach another man, his
equal altogether, but if that other man has the power of attaching
you more, he will be in your eyes the most perfect.

I shall be glad if you *can* revive past feelings, and from your
unbiased self resolve to go on as you have done, but this I do not

expect, and without it I cannot wish you to be fettered. I should not be afraid of your *marrying* him; with all his worth, you would soon love him enough for the happiness of both; but I should dread the continuance of this sort of tacit engagement, with such an uncertainty as there is, of *when* it may be completed. Years may pass, before he is independent; you like him well enough to marry, but not well enough to wait. The unpleasantness of appearing fickle is certainly great — but if you think you want punishment for past illusions, there it is — and nothing can be compared to the misery of being bound *without* love, bound to one, and preferring another. *That* is a punishment which you do *not* deserve . . .

I am to take the Miss Moores back on Saturday, and when I return I shall hope to find your pleasant, little, flowing scrawl on the table. It will be a relief to me after playing at ma'ams for tho' I like Miss H. M. as much as one can at my time of life after a day's acquaintance, it is uphill work to be talking to those whom one knows so little.

Only *one* comes back with me tomorrow, probably Miss Eliza, and I rather dread it. We shall not have two ideas in common. She is young, pretty, chattering, and thinking chiefly (I presume) of dress, company, and admiration . . .

Thank you — but it is not settled yet whether I *do* hazard a 2d edition. We are to see Egerton today, when it will probably be determined. People are more ready to borrow and praise, than to buy — which I cannot wonder at; but tho' I like praise as well as anybody, I like what Edward calls *Pewter* too. I cannot suppose we differ in our ideas of the Christian religion. You have given an excellent description of it. We only affix a different meaning to the word *evangelical*.

Yours most affectionately *J. A*usten

'He' in this letter was John Plumtre.

❝ 'Pray, dear Miss Woodhouse, tell me what I ought to do?'

'I shall not give you any advice, Harriet. I will have nothing to do with it. This is a point which you must settle with your own feelings . . . I lay it down as a general rule, Harriet, that if a woman *doubts* as to whether she should accept a man or not, she certainly ought to refuse him. If she can hesitate as to "Yes," she ought to say "No" directly. It is not a state to be safely entered into with doubtful feelings, with half a heart. I thought it my duty as a friend, and older than yourself, to say thus much to you. But do not imagine that I want to influence you.'

'Oh! no, I am sure you are a great deal too kind to – but if you would just advise me what I had best do – no, no, I do not mean that – as you say, one's mind ought to be quite made up – one should not be hesitating – it is a very serious thing. It will be safer to say "No," perhaps. Do you think I had better say "No?"'

'Not for the world,' said Emma, smiling graciously, 'would I advise you either way. You must be the best judge of your own happiness.' **❞**

EMMA

Emma manipulates her young protégée into refusing an offer of marriage which is attractive to Harriet, but inconvenient to Emma herself.

ABOVE *'The Misses Harriet and Elizabeth Burney' by John Smart, 1806. Playing the piano was an expected accomplishment for young ladies. Caroline Austen remembers her Aunt Jane practising regularly every morning before breakfast: 'She played very pretty tunes.'*

To Caroline Austen

HANS PLACE MONDAY NIGHT OCT: 30 [1815]

My dear Caroline

I HAVE NOT YET FELT quite equal to taking up your manuscript, but I think I shall soon, and I hope my detaining it so long will be no inconvenience. It gives us great pleasure that you should be at Chawton . . . You will practise your music of course, and I trust to you for taking care of my instrument and not letting it be ill used in any respect . . .

I am sorry you got wet in your ride; now that you are become an aunt, you are a person of some consequence and must excite great interest whatever you do. I have always maintained the importance of aunts as much as possible, and I am sure of your doing the same now . . .

Yours affecly *J. Austen*

ABOVE *Music belonging to Jane Austen which can be seen at Chawton. Of the songs her aunt played at Chawton, Caroline Austen's favourite was 'a little French ditty in her manuscript book. The two first lines were,* Que j'aime à voir les hirondelles/Volent ma fenêtre tous les jours.'

LEFT *'Brompton' by George Scharf. This rural scene is as it would have looked when Henry and Eliza first set up house in London.*

To James Stanier Clarke

DEC 11 [1815]

Dear Sir

*M*Y EMMA IS NOW so near publication that I feel it right to assure you of my not having forgotten your kind recommendation of an early copy for C. H. – and that I have Mr. Murray's promise of its being sent to H. R. H. under cover to you, three days previous to the work being really out.

I must make use of this opportunity to thank you dear Sir, for the very high praise you bestow on my other novels. I am too vain to wish to convince you that you have praised them beyond their merit.

My greatest anxiety at present is that this 4th work shd. not disgrace what was good in the others. But on this point I will do myself the justice to declare that whatever may be my wishes for its success, I am very strongly haunted by the idea that to those readers who have preferred P. and P. it will appear inferior in wit; and to those who have preferred M. P., very inferior in good sense. Such as it is, however, I hope you will do me the favour of accepting a copy. Mr. M. will have directions for sending one.

I am quite honoured by your thinking me capable of drawing such a clergyman as you gave the sketch of in your note of Nov. 16. But I assure you I am *not*. The comic part of the character I might be equal to, but not the good, the enthusiastic, the literary. Such a man's conversation must at times be on subjects of science and philosophy of which I know nothing – or at least be occasionally abundant in quotations and allusions which a woman who, like me, knows only her own mother-tongue and has read little in that, would be totally without the power of giving. A classical education, or at any rate, a very extensive acquaintance with English literature, ancient and modern, appears to me quite indispensable for the person who wd. do any justice to your clergyman; and I think I may boast myself to be, with all possible vanity, the most unlearned and uninformed female who ever dared to be an authoress.

Believe me, dear Sir,

Your obliged and faithl. Hum. Serv. *Jane Austen*

'C. H.' was Carlton House; 'H. R. H.', His Royal Highness the Prince Regent.

RIGHT *The Grand Staircase of Carlton House as it would have appeared to Jane on her conducted tour of the Prince's over-lavish residence.*

To Anna Lefroy

PROBABLY [1815] DECEMBER OR EARLY [1816]

My dear Anna

A s I WISH VERY much to see *your* Jemima, I am sure you will like to see *my* Emma, and have therefore great pleasure in sending it for your perusal. Keep it as long as you chuse, it has been read by all here.

BELOW *Post-chaises from Pyne's Microcosm, 1806.*

Jemima, Anna's first child, had been born on 20 October.

To Caroline Austen

CHAWTON. WEDNESDAY MARCH 13 [1816]

My dear Caroline

I AM VERY GLAD TO have an opportunity of answering your agreeable little letter. You seem to be quite my own niece in your feelings towards Mme. de Genlis. I do not think I could even now, at my sedate time of life, read Olympe et Théophile without being in a rage. It really is too bad! Not allowing them to be happy together when they are married. Don't talk of it, pray . . .

I had a very nice letter from your brother not long ago, and I am quite happy to see how much his hand is improving . . .

We have had a great deal of fun lately with post-chaises stopping at the door; three times within a few days we had a couple of agreeable visitors turn in unexpectedly – your Uncle Henry and Mr. Tilson, and Mrs. Heathcote and Miss Bigg, your Uncle Henry and Mr. Seymour. Take notice it was the same Uncle Henry each time . . .

Your affec: Aunt *J. A*usten

To James Stanier Clarke

CHAWTON NEAR ALTON APRIL 1ST [1816]

My dear Sir,

I AM HONOURED BY THE Prince's thanks and very much obliged to yourself for the kind manner in which you mention the work . . .

BELOW *A miniature painted on ivory of the Prince Regent; with some reluctance Jane dedicated* Emma *to the Prince.*

ABOVE AND RIGHT *Domestic life portrayed by John Harden of his family in Westmorland, vividly evoking the Austen's similar domestic life at Chawton and highlighting the ridiculousness of Reverend James Stanier Clarke's suggestion.*

Under every interesting circumstance which your own talent and literary labours have placed you in, or the favour of the Regent bestowed, you have my best wishes. Your recent appointments I hope are a step to something still better. In my opinion, the service of a court can hardly be too well paid, for immense must be the sacrifice of time and feeling required by it.

You are very, very kind in your hints as to the sort of composition which might recommend me at present, and I am fully sensible that an historical romance, founded on the House of Saxe Cobourg, might be much more to the purpose of profit or popularity than such pictures of domestic life in country villages as I deal in – but I could no more write a romance than an epic poem. I could not sit seriously down to write a serious romance under any other motive than to save my life, and if it were indispensable for me to keep it up and never relax into laughing at myself or other people, I am sure I should be hung before I had finished the first chapter. No, I must keep to my own style and go on in my own way; and though I may never succeed again in that, I am convinced that I should totally fail in any other.

I remain my dear Sir,

Your very much obliged, and very sincere friend, *J. Austen*

66 'Mr Darcy is not to be laughed at!' cried Elizabeth. 'That is an uncommon advantage, and uncommon I hope it will continue, for it would be a great loss to *me* to have many such acquaintance. I dearly love a laugh.'

'Miss Bingley,' said he, 'has given me credit for more than can be. The wisest and the best of men, nay, the wisest and best of their actions, may be rendered ridiculous by a person whose first object in life is a joke.'

'Certainly,' replied Elizabeth – 'there are such people, but I hope I am not one of *them*. I hope I never ridicule

Eliza Bennet's candidates for permissible ridicule perhaps reflect those of her creator.

what is wise or good. Follies and nonsense, whims and inconsistencies *do* divert me, I own, and I laugh at them whenever I can. But these, I suppose, are precisely what you are without.'

'Perhaps that is not possible for any one. But it has been the study of my life to avoid those weaknesses which often expose a strong understanding to ridicule.'

'Such as vanity and pride.'

'Yes, vanity is a weakness indeed. But pride – where there is a real superiority of mind, pride will be always under good regulation.' **"**

PRIDE AND PREJUDICE

To John Murray

CHAWTON APRIL 11, 1816

Dear Sir,

I RETURN YOU THE QUARTERLY REVIEW with many thanks. The authoress of Emma has no reason I think to complain of her treatment in it – except in the total omission of Mansfield Park. I cannot but be sorry that so clever a man as the reviewer of Emma should consider it as unworthy of being noticed. You will be pleased to hear that I have received the Prince's thanks for the *handsome* copy I sent him of Emma. Whatever he may think of *my* share of the work, *yours* seems to have been quite right . . .

I remain, dear Sir,

Yours very faithfully *J. A*usten

Sir Walter Scott was the reviewer in question.

CHAWTON AND WINCHESTER
1816–1817

• ● •

Last Days

In May 1816 Edward Austen Knight and Fanny spent a few weeks at Chawton Cottage, probably amusing themselves inventing episodes for Jane's parodic 'Plan of a Novel, according to hints from various quarters' in which Mr. Stanier Clarke's ludicrous proposals were incorporated more or less verbatim.

After the Knights' departure Jane and Cassandra went to Cheltenham in the hope that a course of the spa waters might cure, or at least alleviate, the distressing symptoms from which Jane was suffering. They broke their outward journey at Steventon, returning via the Fowles at Kintbury; and this was to prove Jane's last tour of visits. It is now believed that she was probably suffering from Addison's Disease, or a related affliction of the adrenal glands, producing general weakness and depression, and characterised by such symptoms as the patches of dark and white skin pigmentation that Jane described in a letter. At that time the disease, though usually attended by periods of remission, was ultimately fatal.

By the middle of June the sisters were back at Chawton, and Jane, despite general debility and a sense of discouragement, settled down to her work on *Persuasion*. A manuscript has been preserved of a discarded version of the chapter containing Captain Wentworth's proposal to Anne Elliot, which the novelist rewrote to her satisfaction during a brief interlude of renewed creative energy.

BELOW *Watercolour by Isaac Cruikshank of a woman riding a donkey. In her last months Jane hoped to benefit from such exercise, but her failing strength did not permit this for long.*

Caroline Austen's memories of this time are of her aunt's gradual decline. No longer strong enough for walks, Jane for a while enjoyed rides on her mother's donkey, but soon even these became too much of an effort to be borne. She liked to lie down after dinner, making herself an uncomfortable arrangement of three chairs, because, as Caroline discovered, she was anxious not to deprive Mrs. Austen of the comfort of the only sofa: a small but revealing instance of Jane's sensitive filial care.

Towards the end of the summer Cassandra evidently felt happy enough about her sister's health to leave her for another visit to Cheltenham, this time with the ailing Mary Lloyd, James's wife. Jane meanwhile found solace in the company of the eighteen-year-old Edward Austen, James's son, who amused her, and of whom she became increasingly fond. Her famous description of 'the little bit (two inches wide) of ivory on which I work with so fine a brush, as produces little effect after much labour' appeared in a letter to this same Edward written on her birthday, 16 December 1816, in which she slyly teased him about his current experiment in novel writing.

Henry and Edward senior were frequent visitors at the cottage that winter, and Charles came for a short spell in November, in low spirits after the loss of his ship, the *Phoenix*, off the coast of Asia Minor. Henry was by now ordained, and Jane looked forward to hearing him preach. In the New Year of 1817 a respite from her illness enabled her to spend a few days with the Frank Austens at Alton, which she managed to enjoy in spite of a crowd of unruly children. She then settled to work on the uncompleted novel now known as *Sanditon*, achieving twelve chapters before weakness forced her to abandon it. In March, however, she felt able to write again to Fanny in her own special blend of affection and mockery, attempting to guide her niece through further problems of the heart. Fanny needed to be reassured of the wisdom of having rejected Mr. Plumtre, who had disconcerted her by calmly directing his attentions elsewhere.

BELOW *View of the High Street, Winchester, with plan, from Ball's* Descriptive Walks through Winchester, *1818.*

Mr. Leigh Perrot, now in his eighties, died at the end of March 1817. He left all his property to his widow for her life, causing consternation to his nephews and nieces, who, on the evidence of past kindness, had confidently expected him to leave his sister, Mrs. Austen, well provided for. Mrs. Austen herself remained unperturbed, but the disappointment was too much for Jane's weakened nerves, and she uncharacteristically gave way to a state of despondency which led to a bad physical relapse.

BELOW *Silhouette of the indomitable Mrs. George Austen.*

Caroline remembered her last visit to her aunt, which took place at about this time. She and her sister Anna walked over to Chawton from Wyards, and found Jane in her room: 'She was in her dressing gown and was sitting quite like an invalid in an arm chair – but she got up, and kindly greeted us – and then pointing to seats which had been arranged for us by the fire, she said "There's a chair for the married lady, and a little stool for you, Caroline". It is strange, but those trifling words are the last of her's that I can remember ... I do not suppose we stayed a quarter of an hour; and I never saw Aunt Jane again.'

Although Jane now enjoyed a slight improvement, she was most likely aware, or partly so, of the realities of her condition: and at the end of April she made a short will, leaving everything she possessed, with the exception of two small legacies, to Cassandra. By May she had agreed to move into lodgings in Winchester so as to be near Mr. Lyford, a physician whose advice she trusted. She and Cassandra made the sixteen-mile journey to 8 College Street on 24 May, travelling in James's carriage and accompanied, rather to Jane's anxiety, by Henry and her nephew William Knight riding alongside in the pouring rain.

Two days before their departure Jane had written a long letter to Miss Sharpe, the Godmersham governess with whom she remained on intimate terms, speaking hopefully of recovery, and lovingly of her family's care of her – most especially of Cassandra's devoted nursing. By 27 May she was sufficiently recovered from the journey to Winchester to write to 'dearest

Edward', her much-loved nephew and future biographer, quite in her own dryly humorous manner, but at what cost in painful effort cannot be known. The Mrs. Heathcote referred to in this letter as seeing Jane every day was that same Elizabeth Bigg of the very first letter of 1796, dancing with Mr. Heathcote, who did 'not know how to be particular': a full turning of the wheel as, apart from an undated fragment of about the same period, this was to be Jane's last letter.

Early in June Mary Austen arrived in College Street to help nurse her sister-in-law. It is said that during a crisis Jane turned to her gratefully, saying 'You have always been a kind sister to me, Mary.' To Cassandra, however, she had generally written in critical terms of James's wife, portraying her as unsympathetic and domineering.

Henry and James were now constantly at College Street, and the time came when they felt it their duty to tell Jane of her hopeless condition. She remained resigned and calm, and asked to receive the Sacrament while still able to comprehend its significance; and this was duly administered to her by her two much-loved brothers.

There was one last rally, during which she even dictated a lighthearted rhyme about St. Swithin's Day; but on Friday 18 July, after a brief period of distress, Jane died in Cassandra's arms. She was buried in the north aisle of Winchester Cathedral the following Thursday early in the morning, to avoid disturbing the daily services.

Cassandra's two fine letters to Fanny Knight, full of love and grief, written immediately upon her sister's death, provide a moving account of Jane Austen's last hours and her own depth of feeling. 'It is as if I had lost a part of myself', she wrote.

BELOW *The School Room of Winchester College.*

To James Edward Austen

CHAWTON TUESDAY JULY 9 [1816]

My dear Edward

*M*ANY THANKS. A THANK for every line, and as many to Mr. W. Digweed for coming . . .

I am glad you recollected to mention your being come home. My heart began to sink within me when I had got so far through your letter without its being mentioned. I was dreadfully afraid that you might be detained at Winchester by severe illness, confined to your bed perhaps and quite unable to hold a pen, and only dating from Steventon in order, with a mistaken sort of tenderness, to deceive me. But now, I have no doubt of your being at home, I am sure you would not say it so seriously unless it actually were so.

We saw a countless number of post-chaises full of boys pass by yesterday morng. – full of future heroes, legislators, fools and villains. You have never thanked me for my last letter, which went by the cheese. I cannot bear not to be thanked. You will not pay us a visit yet of course, we must not think of it. Your mother must get well first, and you must go to Oxford and *not* be elected; after that, a little change of scene may be good for you, and your physicians I hope will order you to the sea, or to a house by the side of a very considerable pond. Oh! it rains again . . .

Mary Jane and I have been wet through once already today, we set off in the donkey-carriage for Farringdon . . . We met Mr. Woolls – I talked of its being bad weather for the hay and he returned me the comfort of its being much worse for the wheat . . .

Yours affecly *J. A*usten

BELOW *A view of Winchester from St. Giles' Hill, looking towards the cathedral, where Jane lies buried.*

CHAWTON, SUNDAY SEPT 8 [1816]

BELOW *A charade depicted by Diana Sperling in 1818. Such charades were passionately enjoyed by the Austen family.*

My dearest Cassandra,

I HAVE BORNE THE ARRIVAL of your letter today extremely well; anybody might have thought it was giving me pleasure. I am very glad you find so much to be satisfied with at Cheltenham. While the waters agree, everything else is trifling . . .

Mrs. F. A. seldom either looks or appears quite well. Little Embryo is troublesome I suppose.

Our day at Alton was very pleasant – venison quite right – children well-behaved – and Mr. and Mrs. Digweed taking kindly to our charades, and other games . . . We had a beautiful walk home by moonlight.

Thank you, my back has given me scarcely any pain for many days. I have an idea that agitation does it as much harm as fatigue, and that I was ill at the time of your going, from the very circumstance of your going . . .

Eveng . . . I have a letter from Mrs. Perigord; she and her mother are in London again; she speaks of France as a scene of general poverty and misery, no money, no trade – nothing to be got but by the innkeepers – and as to her own present prospects she is not much less melancholy than before.

I enjoyed Edward's company very much, as I said before, and yet I was not sorry when Friday came. It had been a busy week, and I wanted a few days' quiet, and exemption from the thought and contrivancy which any sort of company gives. Composition seems to me impossible, with a head full of joints of mutton and doses of rhubarb . . .

Yours very affec:ly *J. A*usten

Mrs. Perigord had been Eliza de Feuillide's French servant.

To James Edward Austen

CHAWTON, MONDAY DEC: 16 [1816]

My dear Edward,

ONE REASON FOR MY writing to you now, is that I may have the pleasure of directing to you *Esq.* I give you joy of having left Winchester. Now you may own how miserable you were there; now it will gradually all come out – your crimes and your miseries – how often you went up by the mail to London and threw away fifty guineas at a tavern, and how often you were on the point of hanging yourself, restrained only, as some ill-natured aspersion upon poor old Winton has it, by the want of a tree within some miles of the city.

BELOW *J. Britton's prospect of the city of Winchester, 1827.*

Charles Knight and his companions passed through Chawton about 9 this morning; later than it used to be. Uncle Henry and I had a glimpse of his handsome face, looking all health . . .

I wonder when you will come and see us. I know what I rather speculate upon, but shall say nothing. We think Uncle Henry in excellent looks. Look at him this moment and think so too, if you have not done it before; and we have the great comfort of seeing decided improvement in Uncle Charles, both as to health, spirits and appearance. And they are each of them so agreeable in their different way, and harmonise so well, that their visit is thorough enjoyment.

BELOW *Manydown, home of the Bigg Wither family. Elizabeth and Alethea Bigg were intimate friends of the Austen sisters.*

Uncle Henry writes very superior sermons. You and I must try to get hold of one or two, and put them into our novels; it would be a fine help to a volume; and we could make our heroine read it aloud of a Sunday evening, just as well as Isabella Wardour in the Antiquary is made to read the History of the Hartz Demon in the ruins of St. Ruth – tho' I believe, upon recollection, Lovell is the reader. By the by, my dear Edward, I am quite concerned for the loss your mother mentions in her letter; two chapters and a half to be missing is monstrous! It is well that *I* have not been at Steventon lately, and therefore cannot be suspected of purloining them; two strong twigs and a half towards a nest of my own, would have been something. I do not think however that any theft of that sort would be really very useful to me. What should I do with your strong, manly, spirited sketches, full of variety and glow? How could I possibly join them on to the little bit (two inches wide) of ivory on which I work with so fine a brush, as produces little effect after much labour? . . .

Adieu Aimable! – I hope Caroline behaves well to you.

Yours affecly. *J. Austen*

The Antiquary *was the novel by Sir Walter Scott. Edward's 'two chapters' were from a novel he was writing.*

To Alethea Bigg

CHAWTON: JANUARY 24 [1817]

My dear Alethea,

BELOW *Anna Lefroy's drawing of Chawton Church where Henry Austen was curate at the end of Jane's life, and where Mrs. Austen and Cassandra lie buried.*

I THINK IT TIME THERE should be a little writing between us, though I believe the epistolary debt is on *your* side, and I hope this will find all the Streatham party well, neither carried away by the flood, nor rheumatic through the damps . . . We are all in good health and *I* have certainly gained strength through the winter and am not far from being well; and I think I understand my own case now so much better than I did, as to be able by care to keep off any serious return of illness . . . Our own new clergyman is expected here very soon, perhaps in time to assist Mr. Papillon on Sunday. I shall be very glad when the first hearing is over. It will be a nervous hour for our pew, though we hear that he acquits himself with as much ease and collectedness, as if he had been used to it all his life . . .

I hope your letters from abroad are satisfactory. They would not be satisfactory to *me* I confess, unless they breathed a strong spirit of regret for not being in England . . .

Yours affecly. *J. A*usten

The real object of this letter is to ask you for a receipt, but I thought it genteel not to let it appear early. We remember some excellent orange wine at Manydown . . . I should be very much obliged to you for the receipt . . .

Alethea's sister Catherine was married to the Reverend Herbert Hill, Rector of Streatham in Surrey. Henry Austen had been ordained in December 1816 and appointed curate at Chawton.

To Fanny Knight

CHAWTON FEB 20 [1817]

My dearest Fanny

YOU ARE INIMITABLE, IRRESISTIBLE. You are the delight of my life. Such letters, such entertaining letters, as you have lately sent! – such a description of your queer little heart! – such a lovely display of what imagination does. You are worth your weight in gold, or even in the new silver coinage. I cannot express to you what I have felt in reading your history of yourself, how full of pity and concern and admiration and amusement I have been. You are the paragon of all that is silly and sensible, common-place and eccentric, sad and lively, provoking and interesting. Who can keep pace with the fluctuations of your fancy, the capriccios of your taste, the contradictions of your feelings? You are so odd! – and all the time, so perfectly natural – so peculiar in yourself, and yet so like everybody else!

It is very, very gratifying to me to know you so intimately. You can hardly think what a pleasure it is to me, to have such thorough pictures of your heart. Oh! what a loss it will be, when you are married. Mr. J. W. frightens me. He will have you. I see you at the altar . . .

Do not imagine that I have any real objection, I have rather taken a fancy to him . . . and I like Chilham Castle for you; I only do not like you shd. marry anybody. And yet I do wish you to marry very much, because I know you will never be happy till you are; but the loss of a Fanny Knight will be never made up to me.

Ben and Anna walked here last Sunday to hear Uncle Henry, and she looked so pretty, it was quite a pleasure to see her, so young and so blooming, and so innocent, as if she had never had a wicked thought in her life – which yet one has some reason to

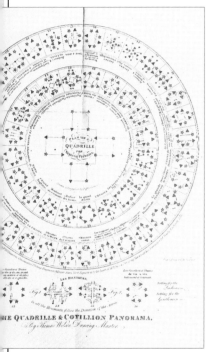

BELOW *A choreographic diagram of the steps of the quadrille from* Wilson's The Quadrille and Cotillion Panorama, *1822.*

suppose she must have had, if we believe the doctrine of original sin, or if we remember the events of her girlish days . . .

Your objection to the quadrilles delighted me exceedingly. Pretty well, for a lady irrecoverably attached to *one* person! – Sweet Fanny, believe no such thing of yourself. Spread no such malicious slander upon your understanding, within the precincts of your imagination. Do not speak ill of your sense, merely for the gratification of your fancy. Yours is sense, which deserves more honourable treatment. You are *not* in love with him. You never have been really in love with him.

Yrs. very affecly *J. Austen*

'Mr. J. W.' was Mr. James Wildman of Chilham Castle, Kent.

To Fanny Knight

CHAWTON, THURSDAY MARCH 13 [1817]

As to making any adequate return for such a letter as yours, my dearest Fanny, it is absolutely impossible, if I were to labour at it all the rest of my life and live to the age of Methuselah, I could never accomplish anything so long and so perfect; but I cannot let William go without a few lines of acknowledgment and reply.

I have pretty well done with Mr. Wildman. By your description, he can*not* be in love with you, however he may try at it, and I could not wish the match unless there were a great deal of love on his side . . .

Poor Mrs. C. Milles, that she should die on the wrong day at last, after being about it so long! – It was unlucky that the Goodnestone party could not meet you, and I hope her friendly, obliging, social spirit, which delighted in drawing people

BELOW *A walking dress showing the parasol carried to protect ladies' complexions from the sun.*

together, was not conscious of the division and disappointment she was occasioning. I am sorry and surprised that you speak of her as having little to leave, and must feel for Miss Milles, though she *is* Molly, if a material loss of income is to attend her other loss. Single women have a dreadful propensity for being poor, which is one very strong argument in favour of matrimony, but I need not dwell on such arguments with *you*, pretty dear, you do not want inclination. Well, I shall say, as I have often said before, do not be in a hurry; depend upon it, the right man will come at last; you will in the course of the next two or three years, meet with somebody more generally unexceptionable than anyone you have yet known, who will love you as warmly as ever *he* did, and who will so completely attract you, that you will feel you never really loved before.

I am got tolerably well again, quite equal to walking about and enjoying the air; and by sitting down and resting a good while between my walks, I get exercise enough. I have a scheme however for accomplishing more, as the weather grows spring like. I mean to take to riding the donkey. It will be more independent and less troublesome than the use of the carriage, and I shall be able to go about with At. Cassandra in her walks to Alton and Wyards . . .

Wm. and I are the best of friends. I love him very much. Everything is so *natural* about him, his affections, his manners and his drollery. He entertains and interests us extremely . . .

Adieu my dearest Fanny . . . The most astonishing part of your character is, that with so much imagination, so much flight of mind, such unbounded fancies, you should have such excellent judgement in what you do! – religious principle I fancy must explain it. Well, good bye and God bless you.

Yrs. very affecly. *J. Austen*

Wyards was Ben and Anna Lefroy's house near Alton.

"Their first meeting in Milsom-street afforded much to be said, but the concert still more. That evening seemed to be made up of exquisite moments. The moment of her stepping forward in the octagon-room to speak to him, the moment of Mr. Elliot's appearing and tearing her away, and one or two subsequent moments, marked by returning hope or increasing despondence, were dwelt on with energy . . .

'I should have thought,' said Anne, 'that my manner to yourself might have spared you much or all of this.'

'No, no! your manner might be only the ease which your engagement to another man would give. I left you in this belief; and yet – I was determined to see you again. My spirits rallied with the morning, and I felt that I had still a motive for remaining here.'

At last Anne was at home again, and happier than any one in that house could have conceived . . . An interval of meditation, serious and grateful, was the best corrective of every thing dangerous in such high-wrought felicity; and she went to her room, and grew steadfast and fearless in the thankfulness of her enjoyment."

PERSUASION

Captain Wentworth and Anne Elliot achieve a happy understanding, as, in due course, would Fanny Knight in her marriage to Edward Knatchbull.

To Anne Sharpe

CHAWTON MAY 22 [1817]

*Y*OUR KIND LETTER MY dearest Anne found me in bed, for in spite of my hopes and promises when I wrote to you I have since been very ill indeed . . . How to do justice to the kindness of all my family during this illness, is quite beyond me! Every dear brother so affectionate and anxious! And as for my sister! – words must fail me in any attempt to describe what a nurse she has been to me . . .

This discharge was on me for above a week, and as our Alton apothecary did not pretend to be able to cope with it, better advice was called in. Our nearest *very good* is at Winchester, where there is a hospital and capital surgeons, and one of them attended me, and *his* applications gradually removed the evil. The consequence is, that instead of going to town to put myself into the hands of some physician, as I shd. otherwise have done, I am going to Winchester instead, for some weeks to see what Mr. Lyford can do farther towards re-establishing me in tolerable health . . .

Mrs. F. A. has had a much shorter confinement than I have – with a baby to produce into the bargain. We were put to bed nearly at the same time, and she has been quite recovered this great while . . .

Adieu. Continue to direct to Chawton, the communication between the two places will be frequent. I have not mentioned my dear mother; she suffered much for me when I was at the worst, but is tolerably well. Miss Lloyd too has been all kindness. In short, if I live to be an old woman, I must expect to wish I had died now, blessed in the tenderness of such a family, and before I had survived either them or their affliction. Sick or well, believe me ever yr. attached friend

J. Austen

BELOW *Visitors being shown a new baby.*

BELOW *An engraving of the choir of Winchester Cathedral.*

Elinor Dashwood devotedly nurses her sister Marianne through a life-threatening illness.

**❝About noon, however, she began – but with a caution – a dread of disappointment, which for some time kept her silent, even to her friend – to fancy, to hope she could perceive a slight amendment in her sister's pulse; she waited, watched, and examined it again and again . . . Her breath, her skin, her lips, all flattered Elinor with signs of amendment, and Marianne fixed her eyes on her with a rational, though languid, gaze.

She continued by the side of her sister with little intermission the whole afternoon, calming every fear, satisfying every inquiry of her enfeebled spirits, supplying every succour, and watching almost every look and every breath. The possibility of a relapse would of course, in some moments, occur to remind her of what anxiety was – but when she saw, on her frequent and minute examination, that every symptom of recovery continued, and saw Marianne at six o'clock sink into a quiet, steady, and to all appearance comfortable, sleep, she silenced every doubt. **"**

SENSE AND SENSIBILITY

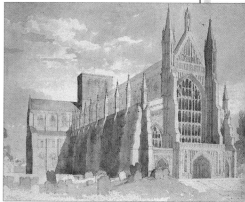

BELOW *Watercolour by John Buckler of Winchester Cathedral.*

To James Edward Austen

MRS. DAVIDS, COLLEGE ST. WINTON TUESDAY MAY 27 [1817]

I KNOW NO BETTER WAY my dearest Edward, of thanking you for your affectionate concern for me during my illness, than by telling you myself as soon as possible that I continue to get better. I will not boast of my handwriting; neither that nor my face have yet recovered their proper beauty, but in other respects I am gaining strength very fast. I am now out of bed from 9 in the morng. to 10 at night – upon the sofa 'tis true – but I eat my meals with Aunt Cassandra in a rational way, and can employ myself and walk from one room to another. Mr. Lyford says he will cure me, and if he fails I shall draw up a memorial and lay it before the Dean and Chapter, and have no doubt of redress from that pious, learned, and disinterested body. Our lodgings are very comfortable. We have a neat little drwg. room with a bow-window overlooking Dr. Gabell's garden. Thanks to the kindness of your father and mother in sending me their carriage, my journey hither on Saturday was performed with very little fatigue, and had it been a fine day I think I shd. have felt none; but it distressed me to see Uncle Henry and Wm. K. who attended us on horseback, riding in the rain almost all the way . . .

We see Mrs. Heathcote every day, and William is to call upon us soon. God bless you my dear Edward. If ever you are ill, may you be as tenderly nursed as I have been. May the same blessed alleviations of anxious, sympathising friends be yours, and may you possess — as I dare say you will — the greatest blessing of all, in the consciousness of not being unworthy of their love. *I* could not feel this.

Your very affec: Aunt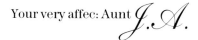

'Winton': a shortened form of Winchester. 'Dr. Gabell': Head-master of Winchester College. 'Wm. K.': Jane's nephew William Knight. 'Mrs. Heathcote': Elizabeth Bigg, widow of the Reverend William Heathcote, Prebendary of Winchester Cathedral, was living in the Close at Winchester with her sister Alethea.

This letter to an unnamed correspondent appeared in the Bio-graphical Notice *prefixed to the first edition of* Northanger Abbey.

[MAY 1817]

*M*Y ATTENDANT IS ENCOURAGING, and talks of making me quite well. I live chiefly on the sofa, but am allowed to walk from one room to the other. I have been out once in a sedan-chair, and am to repeat it, and be promoted to a wheel-chair as the weather serves. On this subject I will only say further that my dearest sister, my tender, watchful, indefatigable nurse, has not been

ABOVE *A coloured aquatint of Winchester College from the Warden's Garden.*

made ill by her exertions. As to what I owe to her, and to the anxious affection of all my beloved family on this occasion, I can only cry over it, and pray to God to bless them more and more . . .

Cassandra Austen to Fanny Knight

WINCHESTER: SUNDAY JULY 18, [1817]

My dearest Fanny,

*D*OUBLY DEAR TO ME now for her dear sake whom we have lost. She did love you most sincerely, and never shall I forget the proofs of love you gave her during her illness in writing those kind, amusing letters at a time when I know your feelings would have dictated so different a style . . .

Since Tuesday evening, when her complaint returned, there was a visible change, she slept more and much more comfortably; indeed, during the last eight-and-forty hours she was more asleep than awake. Her looks altered and she fell away, but I perceived no material diminution of strength, and, though I was then hopeless of a recovery, I had no suspicion how rapidly my loss was approaching.

I *have* lost a treasure, such a sister, such a friend as never can have been surpassed. She was the sun of my life, the gilder of every pleasure, the soother of every sorrow; I had not a thought concealed from her, and it is as if I had lost a part of myself . . .

She felt herself to be dying about half-an-hour before she became tranquil and apparently unconscious. During that half-hour was her struggle, poor soul! She said she could not tell us

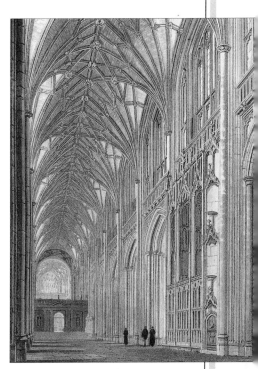

ABOVE *The nave of Winchester Cathedral. Jane Austen's grave is in the north aisle.*

BELOW *Cassandra's silhouette, c.1815. After Jane's death Cassandra wrote: 'If I think of her less as on earth, God grant that I may never cease to reflect on her as inhabiting heaven, and never cease my humble endeavours (when it shall please God) to join her there.'*

what she suffered, though she complained of little fixed pain. When I asked her if there was anything she wanted, her answer was she wanted nothing but death, and some of her words were: 'God grant me patience, pray for me, oh, pray for me!' . . .

Immediately after dinner on Thursday I went into the town to do an errand which your dear aunt was anxious about. I returned about a quarter before six and found her recovering from faintness and oppression; she got so well as to be able to give me a minute account of her seizure, and when the clock struck six she was talking quietly to me.

I cannot say how soon afterwards she was seized again with the same faintness, which was followed by the sufferings she could not describe; but Mr. Lyford had been sent for, had applied something to give her ease, and she was in a state of quiet insensibility by seven o'clock at the latest . . . A slight motion of the head with every breath remained till almost the last. I sat close to her with a pillow in my lap to assist in supporting her head, which was almost off the bed, for six hours, fatigue made me then resign my place to Mrs. J. A. for two hours and a-half, when I took it again, and in about an hour more she breathed her last.

I was able to close her eyes myself, and it was a great gratification to me to render her those last services. There was nothing convulsed which gave the idea of pain in her look; on the contrary, but for the continual motion of the head she gave one the idea of a beautiful statue, and even now, in her coffin, there is such a sweet, serene air over her countenance as is quite pleasant to contemplate.

The last sad ceremony is to take place on Thursday morning; her dear remains are to be deposited in the cathedral . . .

I am, my dearest Fanny,

Most affectionately yours, *Cass. Eliz. Austen*

Cassandra Austen to Fanny Knight

CHAWTON: TUESDAY JULY 29, [1817]

BELOW *Jane's silhouette self-portrait of 1815.*

My dearest Fanny,

I HAVE JUST READ YOUR letter for the third time, and thank you most sincerely for every kind expression to myself, and still more warmly for your praises of her who I believe was better known to you than to any human being besides myself . . . Thursday was not so dreadful a day to me as you imagined. There was so much necessary to be done that there was no time for additional misery . . . I watched the little mournful procession the length of the street; and when it turned from my sight, and I had lost her for ever, even then I was not overpowered, nor so much agitated as I am now in writing of it . . .

I get out of doors a good deal and am able to employ myself. Of course those employments suit me best which leave me most at leisure to think of her I have lost, and I do think of her in every variety of circumstance. In our happy hours of confidential intercourse, in the cheerful family party which she so ornamented, in her sick room, on her death-bed, and as (I hope) an inhabitant of heaven . . .

In looking at a few of the precious papers which are now my property I have found some memorandums, amongst which she desires that one of her gold chains may be given to her goddaughter Louisa, and a lock of her hair be set for you. You can need no assurance, my dearest Fanny, that every request of your beloved aunt will be sacred with me. Be so good as to say whether you prefer a brooch or ring. God bless you, my dearest Fanny.

Believe me, most affectionately yours,

*C*ass. *E*lizth. *A*usten

IN THE FOOTSTEPS OF
JANE AUSTEN

Jane Austen's childhood and youth were spent at Steventon, about six miles west of Basingstoke. Of the parsonage house in which she grew up only the kitchen pump remains, though the outlines of her terraced Elm Walk can be made out just above. The twelfth-century church contains a number of Austen memorials, including a bronze plaque commemorating the novelist. Her baptism is recorded in the parish registers; and under Banns and Marriages there is an entry in her youthful hand of an imaginary marriage between herself and a Henry Frederic Howard Fitzwilliam of London. The neighbourhood abounds in villages and country houses the names of which will be familiar to readers of Jane Austen's letters.

Bath, Jane Austen's second home, retains the glories of its golden stone crescents and squares. On earlier visits Jane had stayed with her Leigh Perrot uncle and aunt at the Paragon, still to be admired today, and on one occasion she lodged in Queen Square. She visited, as will the modern visitor, the Pump Room, with its colonnaded interior, where fashionable Bath gathered to gossip and take the therapeutic waters; danced in the glittering Upper Rooms, now known as the Assembly Rooms; and attended services in the Abbey. The Austens' first settled home in Bath was 4 Sydney Place, in those days on the edge of open country, and overlooking Sydney Gardens, where parties, concerts, and firework displays were enjoyed by Jane and Cassandra. There is a commemorative plaque on the elegant façade of No. 4. Mr. Austen is buried in Walcot Church, where he and Jane's mother had been married. Many of the walks enjoyed by Jane remain, such as that over Sion Hill to Weston taken at such a rattling pace in the company of Mrs. Chamberlayne, with its bird's eye view of Bath far below. In the city, Milsom Street and its surroundings are still lined with tempting shops.

For the pilgrim of Jane Austen who has more than a passing acquaintance with her work, the city is peopled with the shades of characters from *Northanger Abbey* and *Persuasion*. Catherine Morland and the bewitching Henry Tilney saunter down Milsom Street; perfidious Isabella Thorpe ogles the passers by; *Persuasion*'s Anne Elliot hurries to visit poor Mrs. Smith in Westgate Buildings, returning to Sir Walter Elliot's pretentious lodgings in Camden Place (now Camden Crescent), or to Lady Russell's in Rivers Street. The haughty Dalrymples lived in Laura Place – Jane herself would have liked to find lodgings for the family there. Anne's crucial conversation with Captain Wentworth took place in the Octagon Room of the Assembly Rooms, and the lovers' blissful walk of reconciliation began in Union Street.

From Bath the Austens visited Lyme Regis, set in the Dorset countryside so much admired by Jane. Sandstone cliffs crowned with woods ring the little town, and the Cobb is still there from which Louisa Musgrove fell, and along which Jane walked with Miss Armstrong, 'who seems to like people rather too easily'. A cliff garden commemorating the bicentenary of the novelist's birth is on the site traditionally ascribed to the Austens' lodgings.

Jane Austen's six novels were all either revised or written from Chawton Cottage, near Alton. The house has been restored by the Jane Austen Memorial Trust and is now a museum which, with its rich collection of Jane Austen memorabilia, persuasively evokes a living past. The many treasures shown include the topaz crosses given by Charles Austen to his sisters, displayed with Jane's letter telling Cassandra of the gift; the patchwork quilt worked by Mrs. Austen and Jane; and Jane's manuscript music open on the piano. Her donkey carriage is in an outhouse; and flowers mentioned in her letters flourish in the garden. In the church there are monuments to the Knight family, and Mrs. Austen and Cassandra lie buried in the churchyard.

The last months of Jane Austen's life were spent in Winchester at 8 College Street, near the Cathedral Close. A slate plaque commemorates her time in the house. The visitor can stand here and recall how Cassandra watched in the early morning from the first-floor bow window as Jane's funeral procession made its way up the street and out of sight. The slab marking Jane's grave is in the north aisle of the Cathedral nave, with a brass plaque on the wall above it; and there is also a memorial window. The nearby City Museum displays several treasures relating to the novelist.

NOTE TO THIS EDITION

━━━━━━━━━━━━━━━ ● ● ● ━━━━━━━━━━━━━━━

Following the publication of Lord Brabourne's edition in 1884, further letters were published in *Jane Austen's Sailor Brothers* by J. H. Hubback and E. C. Hubback in 1906 and by J. Austen-Leigh and R. A. Austen-Leigh in *Jane Austen, Her Life and Letters: A Family Record* in 1913. In 1932 *Jane Austen's Letters to Her Sister Cassandra and Others*, collected and edited by R. W. Chapman, was published and has since been revised. The editor of the present edition wishes to acknowledge her debt to Dr. Chapman for some of the information in her introductions and notes; also to Park Honan, author of *Jane Austen, Her Life*, 1987, and to the considerable researches of Deirdre Le Faye published in the revised and enlarged version of *Jane Austen, Her Life and Letters: A Family Record*, 1989. *Jane Austen: a Biography* by Elizabeth Jenkins remains one of the most perceptive works on the novelist's life, which no editor can afford to neglect; as is also the case with Mary Lascelles' inimitable *Jane Austen and her Art*.

In 1990 *Jane Austen's Manuscript Letters in Facsimile*, edited by Jo Modert, was published. It contains 'Reproductions of Every Known Extant Letter, Fragment, and Autograph Copy, with an Annotated List of All Known Letters'. This has been used to reinstate words deliberately omitted or incorrectly transcribed in the early editions.

In the main, the style set by Lord Brabourne, making paragraphs, and altering some of her capital letters, and '&' to 'and', has been adhered to. The spelling has been standardised, but apart from omitting the dashes after full points and inserting three dots to indicate omissions, the punctuation, abbreviations and contractions are as in the original manuscripts. Jane Austen's underlinings are indicated by italics. All this has been done in the interests of producing a version of the letters that is easy for the present-day reader to comprehend while retaining the essence of Jane Austen's style of writing. Caroline Mustill has helped to produce this new edition.

In addition to the books already mentioned, the editor has referred, amongst others, to the following works:

AUSTEN, Caroline, *My Aunt Jane Austen*, Jane Austen Society, 1952; AUSTEN-LEIGH, Emma, *Jane Austen and Steventon*, London 1937; *Jane Austen and Bath*, London 1939; AUSTEN-LEIGH, R. A., *Austen Papers 1704–1856*, London 1942; *Jane Austen and Lyme Regis*, London 1946; BUSSBY, Canon F., *Jane Austen in Winchester*, Winchester 1969; CECIL, David, *A Portrait of Jane Austen*, London 1978; CHAPMAN, R. W., *Jane Austen – Facts and Problems*, Oxford 1948; EDWARDS, A-M., *In the Steps of Jane Austen*, Southampton, second edition 1985; FREEMAN, Jean, *Jane Austen in Bath*, Jane Austen Society, 1969; HILL, Constance, *Jane Austen, her Homes and her Friends*, London 1902; JENKINS, Elizabeth, *Jane Austen: a Biography*, London, second edition 1958; LASCELLES, Mary, *Jane Austen and her Art*, Oxford 1939

Present location of the manuscripts of Jane Austen's letters included in this book:

British Library: 54, 55, 57, 77, 83, 86, 97, 101; (on deposit from Joan Austen Leigh): 131, 139, 141, 149; Fitzwilliam Museum, Cambridge: 42; Historical Society of Pennsylvania: 69; Houghton Library, Harvard University: 103 (letter of 14.10.1813); Jane Austen Memorial Trust: 91, 92, 94, 111, 128; Jane Austen Society: 47; Kent County Archives Office (on deposit from Lord Brabourne): 120, 124, 144, 145; Massachusetts Historical Society: 34; Pierpont Morgan Library: 20, 26, 27, 32, 35, 37, 44, 45, 50, 64, 67, 68, 71, 75, 84, 88, 90, 95, 103 (letter of 11.10.1813), 110, 114, 140, 147; Princeton University Library: 73; Privately owned: 22, 29, 33, 126, 130, 151, 153; St. John's College, Oxford: 115, 116, 118; Torquay Natural History Society Museum: 30; Unknown: 18, 19, 23, 25, 56, 62, 65, 70, 133, 143, 150

INDEX

NOTE: Page numbers in *italic* refer to illustration captions.

ACKNOWLEDGEMENTS

— • • —

The illustrations are reproduced by kind permission of the following:
Abbot Hall Art Gallery, Kendal, Cumbria (A. S. Clay Collection): 82, 111;
the great-grandsons of Admiral Sir Francis Austen: 10 (photo Robert
Harding); Jane Austen Memorial Trust: 15, 23, 29, 42–3, 54, 65, 89, 110,
120, 122, 127, 137, 143, 153; Bath Reference Library: 46, 55; Birmingham City Art Gallery: 8 (photo Courtauld Institute); Bridgeman Art
Library: 7, 11; Bristol City Art Gallery: 51 (Bridgeman Art Library);
British Library: 12, 13, 16–17, 21, 58, 60–1, 66–7, 80–1, 83, 95, 108,
110–11, 134, 149; British Museum: front jacket, 52–3 (Fotomas), 127;
Christie's: 48, 52; Courtauld Institute of Art: 8–9 (Spooner Collection),
27 (Witt Collection), 104 (Witt Collection), 136 (Private Collection);
Guildhall Library: 75 (Bridgeman Art Library); Houghton Library, Har-
vard University: 14, 88; Richard Knight: 16, 78, 106 (Bridgeman Art
Library); Laing Art Gallery, Newcastle upon Tyne: 63; Leeds City Art
Gallery: 87 (photo Courtauld Institute); J. G. Lefroy, Carrigglas Manor,
Longford: 18; Philippa Lewis: 31, 56, 67, 100; Mander & Mitchenson
Theatre Collection: 87, 113; Mansell Collection: 34, 74, 76, 94–5, 113,
119, 120; National Gallery of Art, Washington: 68 (Paul Mellon Collection); National Library of Scotland: 132; National Portrait Gallery: back
jacket, 3, 10, 116, 131; Neville Ollerenshaw for Diana Sperling's illustrations in *Mrs. Hurst Dancing*, published by Victor Gollancz: 20, 104, 118,
140; Royal Academy of Dancing, Philip Richardson Collection: 19, 50,
144, 145; Sotheby & Co.: 63, 112, 117, 139; Tate Gallery: 59; Victoria &
Albert Museum: 126 (ET Archive); Victoria Art Gallery, Bath: 17, 32, 33
(photos Courtauld Institute), 43, 47 (Bath Museums Service); Trustees of
the Wedgwood Museum, Barlaston, Staffordshire: 91; Westcountry Stu-
dies Library, Devon Library Services: 40; Jeremy Whitaker: 31; Commander D. P. Willan R.N., D.S.C.: 60, 61; Winchester Central Library: 136–7,
141, 148; Winchester Dean & Chapter: 152; Yale Centre for British Art:
26 (Paul Mellon Collection), 98 (Yale University Art Gallery), 148 (Paul
Mellon Collection).

These illustrations come from the following books and periodicals:
*Bath, illustrated by a Series of Views, from the Drawings of John
Claude Nattes*, London (1806): 2, 37, 38, 45; *La Belle Assemblée, or
Bells Court and Fashionable Magazine*, London (1806–1810): 42, 86;
Botanical Magazine, or Flower Garden Displayed, published by Wil-
liam Curtis, London (1787–1800): 64, 80, 91; *The Costume of Great
Britain, Designed, Engraved and Written by W. H. Pyne*, London
(1808): 8, 24, 42, 90, 123; *Gallery of Fashion*, published by Niklaus
Heideloff, London (1790–1822): 23, 26, 28, 30, 146; *The History of the
Colleges of Winchester, Eton and Westminster*, published by R. Acker-
mann, London (1816): 70, 138–9, 148, 150–1; *The History of the Royal
Residences by W. H. Pyne*, London (1819): 109, 129; *Microcosm, or a
picturesque delineation of the Arts, Agriculture, Manufactures of
Great Britain by W. H. Pyne*, London (1806): 25, 44, 64, 66, 92, 130;
*Orme's Collection of British Field Sports Illustrated from Designs by S.
Howitt*, London (1807): 22, 57, 102, 103; *The Repository of Arts,
Literature, Commerce, Manufacture, Fashions and Politics*, published
by R. Ackermann, London (1809–1828): 35, 69, 84, 85, 91, 94, 99, 114,
115, 119, 124, 125; *Select Illustrations of Hampshire by G. F. Prosser*,
London (1833): 93, 142; *A Treatise on Carriages* by William Felton,
London (1794): 32–3, 48–9, 96, 101; *The World in Miniature, England,
Scotland and Ireland Edited by W. H. Pyne*, London (1827): 36, 122.

EDITOR'S ACKNOWLEDGEMENTS

The editor would like to thank Elizabeth Drury for her expert and
generously sympathetic guidance, and Philippa Lewis for her peerless
picture research. She is grateful to Douglas Matthews, Librarian of the
London Library, for so kindly undertaking the index and to Lucy
Hughes-Hallett for much patient advice.